Banking

William A. Scott

CHAPTER I

The Nature, Functions, and Classification of Banking Institutions

The terms, "bank" and "banking," are applied to institutions and to businesses which differ considerably in character, functions, and methods, but which nevertheless have certain common features which justify their being grouped together. We can best prepare the way for a discussion of these differences and common features by a description of the services which these institutions perform in modern society.

1. Services Performed by Banking Institutions

From the point of view of their customers these services may be grouped under the following heads: The safekeeping of money and other valuables; the making of payments; the making of loans; and the making of investments. It is a common practice everywhere, and in some countries, notably the United States, almost a universal practice for people to intrust their money to banks for safekeeping. To a degree, hoarding, in the sense of locking up money in private vaults and other receptacles and keeping it under the eye and in the personal care of the owner, is still practiced, but it is doubtless on the wane in all civilized countries. The practice of intrusting to banks the safekeeping of other valuables, such as important documents, jewelry, plate, etc., is also widespread and growing.

The service of the safekeeping of money naturally leads to the second, the making of payments. When we intrust our means of payment to a bank, it is natural that we should also make it our treasurer and disbursing agent, and so we do. If we have payments to make to people at home, in other cities of our own country, or in other countries, we usually order our bank to perform the service for us.

Loans of almost all kinds are made by banks, and certain kinds, namely, those to business men for the everyday conduct of commerce and industry, are made almost exclusively by them. For the most part these are short-term loans. For long-term loans banks are also one of the chief resorts, but in some countries these are not to so great a degree monopolized by them as the short-term variety.

For the investment of the surplus funds of people banks are the chief agencies. This function takes the form mainly of the sale of stocks, bonds, and mortgages, and sometimes of the promotion of new enterprises.

None of these services are performed by banks exclusively. For the safekeeping of valuables, and sometimes of money, there are in some places safe deposit companies to which the term "banks" is not applied. In the making of payments the post office departments of governments and express companies participate, and in the making of loans and investments brokers, loan companies, lawyers, etc., participate. The peculiarity of banking institutions consists not in the performance of any one of these services, but in the fact that they specialize in them all, or in a combination of them. Merely to keep money and valuables on deposit, or to act as paymaster, or to make loans, or to sell bonds, stocks, and mortgages would not make an institution a bank or an individual a banker; but to make a business of performing most or all of these services for the public involves the use of certain machinery and certain methods of procedure, and the assumption of a rôle in the nation's economy which is distinctive and peculiar, and which has set these institutions apart in every country as objects of legislation and of scientific treatment, as well as in the thought and regard of the people.

2. The Economic Functions of Banks

Viewed from the standpoint of the nation rather than from that of individuals, the functions of banks may be described as those of intermediaries in exchanges and in the investment of capital. In the former capacity they supply the world with the major part of its medium of exchange and serve as distributing agents for that portion of the supply which comes from other sources. They create a medium of exchange through a process of bookkeeping which is world-wide in extent, and through which the mutual indebtedness of individuals, cities, and other subdivisions of countries and nations, brought about by purchases and sales on credit, are offset without the use of money.

The practice of depositing surplus funds with banks for safekeeping and consequently of using them as paymasters has resulted in the reliance of everybody upon banks for currency in any form, and has thus thrown upon them the responsibility of directly utilizing all the sources of money supply. Thus while the mints of the United States and most other countries coin gold bullion, and supply subsidiary silver and copper and nickel coins to private persons on the same terms as to banks, as a matter of fact few private persons take advantage of this privilege, finding it more convenient and profitable to get the coin they want from banks. The same is true of government notes in countries in which such notes constitute a portion of the currency.

The accumulation of a nation's capital and its investment require the cooperation of numerous agencies of which banks are the chief. They collect the savings of the people, combine them into amounts of sufficient size for investment purposes, and invest them temporarily and sometimes permanently. Cooperating agencies in this work are insurance companies, societies of various kinds for the promotion of saving, stock exchanges, promoters, etc. Some of these take the place of banks in the performance of these services, while others supplement and aid them.

3. Classification of Banking Institutions

Banks differ from one another chiefly in the nature and degree of their specialization, in legal status, and in the place they occupy in the system to which they belong. Some banks devote the major portion of their effort to the conduct of exchanges and are called *commercial* banks, others to investment banking and are called *investment* banks. The most common subclasses under the latter head are savings banks, land or mortgage banks, and bond houses. Savings banks specialize in the collection and investment of small savings; land banks are primarily intermediaries between capitalists and people who wish to invest capital in land, building operations, and agriculture; and bond houses are intermediaries between capitalists and those who wish to invest capital in industrial, commercial, and transportation enterprises, or loan it to states, cities, or other public corporations.

Commercial banks rarely confine themselves exclusively to the conduct of exchanges. Most of them also conduct savings departments and invest the funds intrusted to them through such departments in agricultural, industrial, or commercial enterprises or loan them to public corporations. Commercial banking, however, is their main concern, their other departments being side issues of greater or less importance according to circumstances. Investment banks also frequently carry on commercial banking as a side issue. These two lines of business are sometimes mixed in such proportions as to render classification difficult.

From a legal point of view the banks of nearly all countries may be classified as *private* or unincorporated, and *incorporated*, sometimes also called joint-stock banks. Private banks are started by individuals or firms, like any other private enterprise, without the formality of application for permission to some public officer, and without compliance with a set of legally prescribed regulations. They are subject to the laws of the country governing all kinds of private business enterprises and sometimes to special laws applying specifically to them. In some of the states of the United States such banks are prohibited by law.

Incorporated banks are usually started by private initiative but owe their actual legal existence and status to a special law, to the requirements of which they must conform before they are permitted to do business. Their right to do business is usually evidenced by a document known as a charter, executed and delivered by a public officer legally endowed with the requisite authority, or passed in the form of a law by the legislative organs of the state. Charters of the latter kind are known as special charters and are rarely used nowadays, except in the case of institutions of a peculiar character, endowed with special functions. The central banks of Europe owe their existence to such charters, as did also the first and second United States banks. In the early history of the United States special charters were uniformly employed

6

by the states, but for many years general incorporation laws have been the rule, on compliance with the requirements of which persons who desire to incorporate banks can secure charters.

In federal states, both the federal government and the governments of the constituent states frequently have and exercise the right to incorporate banks. In the United States, banks incorporated by the federal government under the terms of a general law, originally passed in 1863 and many times amended since that date, are known as *national* banks, and those incorporated by the states under the terms of general banking acts or of general incorporation laws are known as *state* banks. These latter are endowed with privileges which enable them to exercise commercial and some investment banking functions. Other banks also are incorporated by our states under the terms of general laws, which are known as savings banks and trust companies. The former, as the name implies, are institutions primarily designed for the encouragement, collection, and investment of savings. The latter are called trust companies because the earliest institutions of this type made the execution of trusts of various kinds their exclusive business. Banking functions were later added and in many cases have now assumed chief importance.

The nature of the banking business requires some kind of organization of the individual institutions in which certain ones will assume to a degree at least the rôle of bankers' banks. In most European countries this position is occupied by single institutions specially chartered and endowed with special privileges and usually described as central banks. Examples are the Bank of England in England, the Bank of France in France, and the Imperial Bank of Germany in Germany. Around these are grouped the other institutions in a kind of hierarchy, certain large banks in the larger cities forming centers about which smaller institutions group themselves. In the United States there is no single central institution, but a small group of banks in New York City are the real centers of the system. Around these are grouped the banks in the other large cities of the country and these in turn perform important services for banks in the surrounding smaller towns and country districts.

CHAPTER II

The Nature and Operations of Commercial Banking

In the preceding chapter commercial banking has been defined as the conduct of exchanges by means of a world-wide process of bookkeeping. We must now describe this process. Its essential features are the discount of commercial paper, the conduct of checking accounts, and the issue of notes.

1. Commercial Paper

By commercial paper is meant the credit instruments or documents which the credit system now in general use throughout the commercial world regularly brings into existence and liquidates.

The essence of this system is buying and selling *on time*. The farmer buys seed, implements, fertilizer, labor, etc., and pays for them after the crops have been harvested and sold. The manufacturer buys raw materials and pays for them after they have passed through the transformation process which he conducts and the completed goods have been marketed. He frequently sells them to jobbers or wholesalers on time and these in turn sell them on time to retailers and these to consumers. Farmers, manufacturers, and merchants both buy on time and sell on time, and are thus both debtors and creditors, and each expects that his sales will ultimately pay for his purchases.

The obligations involved in these transactions are represented and recorded in the form of book accounts, promissory notes, or bills of exchange, the latter being written or printed, or partly written and partly printed, orders of creditors on debtors to pay to themselves or to third parties the sums indicated. These documents are being constantly made and constantly paid as the processes of agriculture, industry, and commerce proceed. Indeed, their creation and liquidation is a normal phenomenon of our modern economic life.

The term commercial paper, as we are using it, applies to such promissory notes and bills of exchange as belong to this credit system. It does not apply to such notes and bills when they owe their existence to credit operations of a different kind, such for example as accommodation loans or investment operations. Indeed, the essential characteristic of commercial paper is not revealed in the form of the credit document but in the fact that it is a link in this chain of exchange operations by which modern commerce is carried on.

This use of the term should also be distinguished from the one common among bankers and others. In this popular usage these documents are called commercial paper because they are themselves objects of commerce. In our use of the term the adjective "commercial" applies to them only when they play the rôle of intermediary in a process of exchange through credit. In this sense it is a matter of indifference whether they pass through the hands of brokers or not, and the fact of their being objects of purchase and sale does not confer the quality of commercial paper upon documents having an origin and character other than that above described.

2. The Operation of Discount

Every person in this chain of credit is confronted with the problem of paying his debts as they mature by the use of the amounts due him from other people. Since it is rarely possible to arrange maturities on both sides in such a way that the amounts due to be paid him at a given date shall at least equal those he is due to pay on that date, some means of transforming claims against other people due in the future into present means of payment must be found. The one universally employed is the discount of commercial paper. By this is meant the exchange at a bank of his own promissory notes due at times when debts of equal or greater amount due him mature, or of bills of exchange drawn against his debtors, for cash or credits on a checking account. These latter are available as means of payment at any time.

As a consideration for this accommodation, the bank charges interest for the period intervening before the maturity of the paper discounted. Sometimes this charge is paid at the time the paper is purchased and sometimes at the date of its maturity. The term "discount" technically means taking interest in advance by making available as means of present payment in any of the above mentioned forms a sum less than the amount the bank expects to collect at the date of the maturity of the discounted paper. If the interest is paid when the discounted paper matures, the process is technically called a loan. However, since the time of collecting interest makes no essential difference in the nature of the transaction, the process is commonly described as the discount of commercial paper, regardless of whether the interest is collected in advance or not.

3. The Conduct of Checking Accounts

A checking account is an ordinary book account on which are credited the cash deposited by a customer and the proceeds of collections, loans, and discounts made on his behalf, and on which are debited payments made to him in cash or on his behalf to other people or to the bank itself. These payments are made on orders signed by the customer and known as checks.

The ordinary customer of a commercial bank every day brings to the bank the cash he receives as the result of the day's business, and the checks received, drawn on his own and other banks, and is credited with the amount on the books of the bank as well as on a passbook which he himself retains. If he needs cash during the day, he presents to the bank a check payable to himself for the amount needed, and receives the kinds and denominations wanted; and if he wants to make payments to his creditors in other forms than cash, he sends them checks on his bank payable to their order, or a check drawn by his bank on some bank in another place, usually called a draft, which he has obtained by exchanging for it a check drawn to the order of his bank. To the amount of these payments his account at the bank is debited, and from time to time his passbook is left at the bank for the entry therein of the debits made to date and its subsequent return to him.

The customer must take care that his account is not overdrawn, that is, that the debits on his account do not exceed the credits, since overdrafts, except by accident or for very short periods and small amounts, are not allowed in this country, and in other countries, where they are allowed, they must be provided for in advance by a special agreement between the bank and the customer, which usually involves the deposit with the bank of ample security. In order to avoid overdrafts, the customer in this country agrees with his banker on what is known as a "line," that is, a maximum amount of loans or discounts to be allowed. Whenever his credit balance falls to a certain minimum, also established by agreement with the bank, the latter discounts for him the paper of his customers, that is, bills of exchange drawn on them or their promissory notes in his favor, or his own promissory notes. The proceeds of these discounts are credited on his account like deposits of cash or of checks for collection.

So long as the discounts are confined to commercial paper the bank's part in these transactions consists almost exclusively of bookkeeping between its customers and between itself and other banks. Ordinarily, what is debited on one man's account is credited on another's, the cash received nearly balancing that paid out. To the extent that the cash receipts and payments do not balance, the bank either has a surplus or is obliged to provide for the meeting of a deficit. The means available for this latter purpose will be explained in subsequent sections, as well as some of the details of this bookkeeping process. For the present it is important to note precisely how the discount of commercial paper is related to this bookkeeping process.

As explained in Section 1, commercial paper is an essential part of the process of exchanging goods through credit. A person buys on time and sells on time and expects to pay for his purchases by the proceeds of his sales. So long, therefore, as the processes of commerce and industry proceed in a normal fashion, the paper discounted by a bank will be paid at maturity and the credit balance created by means of such discounts offset by corresponding debits. Ordinarily the credits created through discounts during a given period, say a day or a week, in favor of one set of customers will be balanced during this same period by the payment of notes previously discounted for other customers. Within a complete trading area this is certain to happen, since purchases and sales of goods are equal and what is credited to one man is debited to another.

11

The result is very different if a bank discounts investment paper, that is, credit documents which represent the unproductive consumption of individuals or of public and private corporations, or which represent the purchase on time of the instruments of production rather than the production of goods through the use of such instruments and their transfer from the producer to the consumer. The means of payment of such documents can only be created gradually by the application of the profits of the enterprises in which the investments were made, or by taxes spread over a series of years, or by a slow process of saving. If a bank issues its own demand obligations in exchange for such documents, it cannot make its books balance and it will be constantly exposed to the danger of forced liquidation. If it attempts to protect itself by requiring that the discounted paper shall mature in a short period, the necessity of liquidation will be forced upon customers who are responsible for the payment of the discounted paper; that is, such customers will be obliged to sell at such prices as they can command the property in which the investments were made, or some other property. Such liquidation always results in forced readjustments of prices and business depression, and sometimes in commercial crises.

4. The Issue of Notes

As an alternative for or a supplement to the conduct of checking accounts a commercial bank may issue its promissory notes payable to bearer on demand. By the issue of notes is meant their transfer to customers in exchange for cash, for checks left for collection or drawn against a credit balance in a checking account, or for discounted notes and bills.

By the use of these notes commercial banking can be carried on without checking accounts. In that case the notes are issued in exchange for cash and discounted bills, and notes are returned to the bank in exchange for cash or when discounted bills or notes mature and are paid. In the bookkeeping process which has been described bank notes thus issued and returned perform precisely the same function as checking accounts, and are related to the discount of commercial paper and the credit system of the

12

country in precisely the same manner as such accounts.

Most banks of issue at the present time conduct checking accounts also, using the one instrumentality or the other as their customers desire. In this case notes are issued in exchange for checks drawn against credit balances on checking accounts or deposited for collection as well as in exchange for discounted notes and bills and cash.

By the use of both notes and checking accounts, a bank can supply most of the needs of its customers for a circulating medium, the notes serving as hand-to-hand money, and the checking accounts, practically all other purposes. Being the direct obligations of banks attested by the signatures of their responsible officers, and being payable to bearer on demand and capable of being issued in all necessary denominations, such notes can be transferred without indorsement, can be used for making change and payments of small and moderate size for which checks are not convenient, and they do not need to be presented at a bank for the test of their validity. If the bank or banks which issue them are properly conducted and supervised and properly safeguarded by law, such notes will circulate freely through the length and breadth of a country.

Checking accounts meet in the most satisfactory manner all currency needs for which hand-to-hand money is not well adapted, such as large payments and payments at a distance. With a few strokes of a pen payments of the greatest magnitude can be made through their agency. Checks can be sent through the mails at slight expense and without danger of loss of the amount involved. By the devices known as travelers' and commercial letters of credit, checking accounts supply the most convenient form of currency for travelers and for merchants engaged in foreign trade.

Besides bank notes and checking accounts the only forms of currency needed in any community are standard and subsidiary coins, the former for use as ultimate redemption material for all other forms of currency and for the payment of international and other balances, and the latter for small change. Even these forms of currency are supplied by commercial banks, but since they do not create them, ways and means of procuring them in the quantities needed constitute one of their peculiar problems.

5. Collections

One of the most important functions of commercial banks is the collection for their customers of checks and drafts drawn on other institutions. When these documents are received, the accounts of customers who deposited them are credited with the amounts, less a small fee for collection, unless by agreement this service of collection is performed free of charge. The checks are then assorted according to the banks upon which they are drawn and the cities in which those banks are located.

Checks drawn upon home banks are collected either through messengers who present the checks at the counters of the banks upon which they are drawn and secure payment therefor, or through the local clearing house. This is a place where representatives of the banks meet for the exchange of checks. After the representative of each bank has distributed all the checks held by his institution against the others participating in the clearing, and received from them those drawn against his bank, a balance sheet is prepared showing the balance due by or to his bank after the total of the checks distributed has been balanced against the total received. If said balance is adverse, it is paid to the master of the clearing house, and if it is favorable, it is received from him.

The checks received through the clearing house or presented by messengers from other banks and paid, are debited to the accounts of the persons who drew them and returned to such persons as vouchers, the net result of the entire transaction being the same as if all the parties involved had been customers of a single bank, with the exception that some means of paying balances had to be found. Since balances are sometimes paid by checks on some central institution in which credit balances may be obtained by rediscounts of commercial paper, this necessity can be met without the use of any form of currency other than that furnished by banks themselves.

Checks drawn upon out-of-town banks are, in this country, collected through so-called correspondents. Each bank enters into an arrangement with a few other banks, distributed throughout the country and conveniently located for the purpose, by which the correspondent bank agrees to conduct

14

with it a checking account on which it will credit at par or at a stipulated discount the checks sent it for collection and debit checks drawn against such an account. A comparatively small number of such correspondents suffices, since certain banks in the larger cities, by making a business of such collections, conduct checking accounts with a large number of banks, and can thus make collections by mere transfers of credits on their own books or by the use of the local clearing house. The so-called reserve cities in this country constitute clearing centers for the territories contiguous to them, and New York, Chicago, and St. Louis, for the entire country.

Checks received from correspondents and drawn against themselves are debited to the accounts of the customers who drew them and returned as vouchers in the same manner as checks received through the clearing house or paid over their own counters.

Through this interchange of checks between banks and the conduct of checking accounts with each other, intermunicipal and international exchanges are conducted through the bookkeeping processes of commercial banks with the same ease and economy as are exchanges between people living in the same town.

6. Domestic Exchange

The accounts of a bank with its correspondents are a record of the transactions of its customers with the outside world, the checks they receive as a result of sales to outsiders of merchandise, real estate or other property, or as a result of gifts by outsiders to them being credited on such accounts, while the checks they draw or the drafts they purchase in payment for merchandise, real estate or other property purchased of outsiders, or of gifts made to them are debited. When in a given period, say a day or a week, the receipts of the customers of a bank from outsiders, as a result of current or past sales and gifts, exceed the payments made by them as a result of purchases and gifts, its credit balances with its correspondents will increase, and under opposite conditions they will decrease. If the payments should continue in excess for a considerable period, the credit balances of a bank

15

with its correspondents would be exhausted and some means of replenishing them would have to be found, and under the opposite conditions too large a portion of the bank's resources would accumulate with its correspondents and some means of withdrawing funds would have to be found.

When a bank needs to replenish its credit balances with its correspondents, it may ship cash or purchase drafts from other home banks, which it can send to its correspondents for collection like checks deposited in the ordinary course of business. The latter resource will of course be available only when these other banks' balances with their correspondents are not exhausted. Should the balances of all the banks of a town with their out-of-town correspondents be nearly or quite exhausted, shipments of cash to correspondents could not be avoided. If a bank wishes to withdraw funds from its correspondents for home use, it may order cash shipped or it may, perhaps, be able to sell drafts for cash to other home banks.

The expenses involved in shipments of cash, loans, or purchases or sales of drafts for the purpose of replenishing balances with or withdrawing them from out-of-town correspondents, give rise to what is called the *rate of exchange*. If, in order to make out-of-town payments for its customers, a bank is obliged to pay the expense of shipping cash to its correspondents or to pay a premium on drafts purchased from other banks, the natural method of reimbursement will be a premium charge on drafts sold equal to the amount of the expense incurred. If it wishes to withdraw a balance with its correspondent, since to order cash shipped will involve expense, it will be glad to sell drafts for cash at a discount not to exceed such expense.

The rate of exchange, or the price of drafts on a given point, may, therefore, fluctuate between a premium equal to the cost of shipping cash to that point and a discount of the same amount. Beyond these extremes, these fluctuations cannot ordinarily go, because customers may demand cash of their banks in payment of checks against their own credit balances and ship it to their out-of-town creditors at their own expense, and would do so if the rates charged on drafts should make such procedure profitable. The actual rate of exchange will not ordinarily reach either of these extremes, on account of competition either between the banks which are desirous of selling drafts on their correspondents or between those which are forced to buy as an alternative to cash shipments. If the aggregate balances of the banks of a town with their out-of-town correspondents are large and increasing, the pressure to sell drafts will be greater than that to buy and the rate of exchange will go to a discount, the amount of which, however, will be fixed by competition between the selling banks. In the opposite case, the rate will go to a premium and be fixed by competition between the buying banks.

In most towns in the United States there is little or no competition between banks in the business of buying and selling drafts and consequently no open market for exchange and no quotations of exchange rates. In such cases each bank acts more or less independently; shipments of cash to or from correspondents are the ordinary means of regulating balances; and the cost of such shipments are charged to the general expense account of the bank and taken out of customers either by a fixed and more or less invariable charge on drafts sold, or in other ways.

Since the balances of the banks of a town with their out-of-town correspondents depend primarily upon the commercial and gift relations of their customers with the outside world, it is pertinent to inquire whether as a result of a long continued excess of purchases from outsiders over sales to them and of gifts to over gifts from them, the cash resources of a community might not be completely exhausted, and if not, how such an outcome is prevented.

Bankers have no direct control over the purchases and sales of their customers, but through the rate of interest they charge on loans and discounts and their ability absolutely to discontinue such accommodations they exert a very potent indirect influence. The rates of interest and discount charged are an important element in the cost of doing business and, if loaning and discounting is discontinued, sales of property to meet maturing obligations are forced, with the result of price readjustments between the town in question and the outside world which speedily change the relations between purchases and sales.

When the cash resources of the banks of a town approach the limit of safety and their balances with their correspondents fall to an ominously low point, the normal method of procedure is to raise the rates on loans and discounts, and if conditions grow worse, to raise them higher still and as a last resort to cease temporarily to make them at any price. By increasing the cost of doing business this rise in the rates will check purchases by diminishing or annihilating the profits resulting, and will stimulate sales by rendering it more profitable for some customers to secure funds by sales to outsiders at lower prices than were formerly asked rather than by borrowing from banks. Under ordinary circumstances this procedure will be sufficient to change an unfavorable into a favorable balance of indebtedness with the outside world, with the result that more checks on outside institutions will be deposited with the banks and a smaller amount of drafts purchased. Bankers' balances with their correspondents will, therefore, increase, and with them their ability to command cash in case of need. The demands made upon them for cash will also decrease, since the volume of loans and of business transacted will fall.

If the banks stop discounting, a more or less violent readjustment with the outside world results. Business men who have obligations to meet, and most of them will belong to this class, are obliged to sell their goods and property at whatever prices are necessary and to stop purchasing entirely. The outcome, so far as the banks are concerned, is as above indicated. If conditions are such that sales at any price cannot be forced, a crisis ensues; that is, business operations are temporarily suspended and transfers of property in settlement of obligations are made through bankruptcy and other court proceedings.

7. Foreign Exchange

The business relations between banks located in different countries do not differ in any essential respect from those between banks located in the same country. Interchange of checks, the conduct of checking accounts, shipments of cash, and borrowing and lending proceed in the same manner as between domestic institutions. The chief peculiarities of the foreign exchanges are due to the fact that different units of value and sometimes different standards must here be reckoned with, and that the precious metals, chiefly gold, are used in the settlement of balances. Drafts drawn in the

United States on English points, for example, call for the payment of pounds sterling, those on French points for francs, and those on German points for marks, while all must be paid for in dollars.

The translation of the language of values of one country into that of others thus involved requires the calculation of a so-called *par of exchange*. By this is meant the relation between the weights of pure metal contained in their respective units of value, if the countries in question have the same standard, and the relation between the market values of the metallic content of their units, if their standards are different. Thus the par of exchange between this country and England is $4.8665, since our dollar contains 23.22 grains of pure gold and the English pound sterling 4.8665 times as many grains, or 113.0016. Our par of exchange with France is 19.294 cents, the quotient of 4.4802, the number of grains of pure gold in the French franc, divided by 23.22. Between China and the United States the par of exchange is the market value in our dollars of the amount of silver contained in the tael, the Chinese unit.

Another technical term employed in connection with the foreign exchanges is *the gold points*. These are the points above and below the par of exchange fixed by the addition in the one case, and the subtraction in the other, of the cost of shipping gold between the two places in question. They are the points between which the rates of exchange fluctuate, or the points at which, when the rate of exchange reaches them, gold moves between gold standard countries. Assuming for example, that the cost of shipping gold between New York and London is two cents per pound sterling, the gold points are 4.8865 and 4.8465, it being profitable to ship gold from New York to London when sterling exchange reaches the former figure and to import gold from London when it reaches the latter figure.

In the conduct of the foreign exchanges several classes of bills are employed upon which the quotations differ, in part on account of differences in their quality and in part on account of the interest element entering into the value of time bills. For example, New York regularly quotes on London *cables, demand,* and *sixty-day* bills. The rates on a certain date were: Cables, 4.8860; demand, 4.8790; and sixty days, 4.8370. Inasmuch as these are all bankers' bills and consequently of the same quality, the differences in their quotations are due to the interest element and to the fact that in the case of the cables the cost of the cablegram is included.

When a New York banker sells a cable on London, his balance with his correspondent is reduced by the amount in a few hours, and the interest he receives on such balances is proportionately diminished at once, and he is also out the cost of the necessary cablegram. When he sells a demand bill, his account with his London correspondent remains undiminished during the time required for sending the bill by mail across the Atlantic and for its presentation for payment. He draws interest on his entire balance during this period. When he sells a sixty-day bill, his balance does not suffer diminution on its account for sixty days. In order to place these bills on a footing of equality so far as he is concerned, therefore, he must quote demand and sixty-day bills lower than cables; the former by the cost of the cablegram plus interest on the amount of the bill, say for ten days, at the rate he receives on his London balance, and the latter by the amount of the cablegram plus interest on the amount for sixty days at the same rate.

Trade, or mercantile, as well as bankers' bills are also frequently and, in some markets, regularly quoted. Being of a quality ranked as inferior to bankers' bills, they must be negotiated at a lower rate and are quoted accordingly.

CHAPTER III

The Problems of Commercial Banking

The conduct of commercial banking presents problems both to the bankers and to the public, the methods of solution of which will be given attention at this point. The problems concerning the bankers primarily may be grouped under the heads, supply of cash, selection of loans and discounts, and rates; and those which primarily concern the public may be grouped under the heads, protection against unsound practices, and adequacy and economy of service.

1. The Supply of Cash

The credit balances on checking accounts and the notes of commercial banks are payable on demand in the legal-tender money of the nation to which they belong, and such banks must at all times be prepared to meet these obligations.

The term employed to designate the funds provided for this purpose is *reserves*, and in this country they consist of money kept on hand and of credit balances in other banks. In other countries there is also included under this head commercial bills of the kind which can always be discounted. The term *secondary reserve* is sometimes employed in this country to designate certain securities, such as high-class bonds listed on the stock exchanges, which can be sold readily for cash in case of need.

The amount of reserve required can be determined only by experience. In ordinary times it depends chiefly upon the habits of the community in which the bank is located regarding the use of hand-to-hand money as distinguished from checks and upon the character of its customers. These habits differ widely in different nations, and considerably in the different sections and classes of the same nation. In most European and Oriental countries, for example, checks are little used by the masses of the people, while in the United States and England they are widely used. In these latter countries, however, they are less widely used by people in the country than in the cities, and by the laboring than the other classes in the cities. Within the same city one bank may need to keep larger reserves than another on account of the peculiarities of the lines of business carried on by its customers and the classes of people with whom it deals.

In times of crisis and other periods of extraordinary demand, bank reserves must be much larger than in ordinary times. Hoarding, unusually large shipments of money to foreign countries and between different sections of the same country, and payments of unusual magnitude, increase the demands for cash made upon banks at such times.

The manner in which clearing and other balances between banks are met also has an influence on the amount of reserves required. If such balances are paid daily and always in cash, the amount needed for this purpose is much larger than if they are paid in checks on some one or a few institutions and at longer intervals.

The note issue privileges of a bank also affect its reserve requirements. Since, if not prohibited by law, notes may be issued in all denominations needed for hand-to-hand circulation within a nation, and since for all purposes except small change such notes are as convenient as any other form of currency, a bank with unrestricted issue privileges can supply all the demands of its customers for currency for domestic use, except those for small change, without resort to outside sources of supply. In this case, however, it needs to keep a reserve in order to meet demands for the redemption of notes. Such demands arise on account of the need of coin for small change or for shipment abroad or of means for meeting domestic clearing and other bank balances. The aggregate needed for the supply of such demands, however, is much less than would be required if the privilege of issuing notes did not exist.

In the maintenance of reserves the chief reliance of commercial banks is the circulation of standard coin within a nation and the importation of such coin. The coin within the borders of a nation passes regularly into the vaults of banks by the process of deposit, and on account of the credit balances they carry with foreign institutions, the loans they are able to secure from them, the commercial paper they hold which is discountable in foreign markets, and the bonds and stocks sometimes in their possession which are salable there, they are able to import large quantities in case of need. Since the standard coin in existence in the world adjusts itself to the need for it in substantially the same manner that the supply of any other instrument or commodity adjusts itself to the demand, banks ordinarily have no difficulty in supplying their needs, and under extraordinary circumstances, though difficulties along this line sometimes arise, means of overcoming them are available which will be discussed in the proper place.

If, as is the case in the United States, certain forms of government notes are available as bank reserves, these find their way into the banks' vaults by the process of deposit in the same manner as coin. The possession of such notes by a bank enables it, to the extent of their amount, to throw the responsibility for the supply of standard coin upon the government, and in the circulation of the country such notes take the place of an equivalent amount of standard coin. Whether or not a government ought to assume such a responsibility is a question which will be discussed in a subsequent chapter.

For the nation as a whole, the balances in other banks and the discountable commercial paper and bonds which a bank may count as a part of its reserves are not reserves except to the extent that they may be employed as a means of importing gold. They are only means through which real reserves of standard coin are distributed. The payment in cash of a balance with another bank or the discount of commercial paper with another domestic bank or the sale of bonds on domestic stock exchanges do not add to the sum total of the cash resources of the banks of a nation. Their only effect is to increase the cash resources of one bank at the expense of another.

Adequate facilities for the distribution of the reserve funds of a country, however, are second in importance only to the existence of adequate supplies of standard coin. If such facilities are lacking, existing reserves can be only partially and uneconomically used, with the result that much larger aggregate reserves are required than would otherwise be necessary and that the entire credit system is much less stable than it otherwise would be.

2. The Selection of Loans and Discounts

The problem of the reserves is vitally connected with that of the selection of loans and discounts. As was shown in the preceding chapter, the chief business of a commercial bank is to conduct exchanges by a process of bookkeeping between individuals, banks, communities, and nations. This process consists primarily in the converting of commercial bills and notes into credit balances and bank notes, in the transfer of such balances and notes between individuals and banks, and in the final extinguishment of such balances and the return of such notes at the maturity of the commercial bills and notes in which the process originated.

In this process there is little need for cash, provided the arrangements between banks for clearing checks and for the interchange of notes are complete and efficiently administered. But when a bank accepts investment in lieu of commercial paper, its need for cash at once increases, because the demand obligations created by the credit balances or the bank notes into which this paper was converted are not extinguished by payments for goods purchased, but must be met by cash.

To distinguish between commercial and investment paper is, therefore, one of the chief problems confronting commercial bankers. For its solution an accurate knowledge of the business operations of customers is necessary. An inspection of the paper presented and a general knowledge of their wealth and business capacity are important, but not sufficient. The forms of the paper employed in both commercial and investment operations may be the same, and the possession of wealth does not ensure the payment of the paper at maturity.

The chief means available for the acquisition of this knowledge are the requirement from customers of frequent statements of their operations, on properly prepared forms; the use, wherever possible, of the documented commercial bill of exchange; and the maintenance of credit departments equipped with the means of accurately studying commercial, industrial, and agricultural operations, and of diagnosing economic conditions. The study of carefully prepared statements of customers made at frequent intervals reveals to the banker not only the nature of the operations represented by the paper presented for discount, but the trend of the business of his customers and, through them, of the entire country. With such knowledge, he is not only able to protect his institution against improper loans and discounts, but to give valuable advice to his customers, advice which no one else is in a position to give so accurately.

By a documented bill of exchange is meant a bill drawn by a seller upon the purchaser of goods, accompanied by documents evidencing the transaction; such, for example, as bills of lading, warehouse receipts, and insurance policies. The names on such bills guide the banker in his efforts to trace the transaction in which it originated and the documents enable him absolutely to identify it, and constitute security for the loan.

Instead of such bills, promissory notes made payable to banks are commonly used in this country, greatly to the disadvantage of the banking business. Such a note reveals nothing to the banker concerning the purpose for which the loan is made, while a commercial bill, even without documents, reveals the names of the principals of the transaction in which the banker is asked to participate. Acquaintance with these men and knowledge of the business in which they are engaged at once suggests the probable origin of the bill and furnishes the clue needed for subsequent investigation.

A properly equipped credit department will keep on file and at all times available for use the data requisite for the information of the officers upon whom the responsibility of selecting the loans and discounts rests. Such data will not only concern the character and business of each customer and the bank's previous dealings with him, but general economic conditions, the operations and experiences of other banks, other business institutions, governments, etc.

3. Rates

Besides rates of exchange considered in the preceding chapter, commercial banks are concerned with loan and discount rates.

Rates on deposits, though sometimes employed, have no place in commercial banking, since commercial deposits are only the credit balances resulting from loans and discounts or from funds intrusted to the bank for temporary safekeeping or disbursement in the interest of the depositor. In every case they represent a service rendered the depositor for which the bank must be paid, and, when interest is allowed, the depositor must repay it in some form with an increment sufficient to remunerate said service.

Commercial banks may and usually do conduct savings accounts also, for which an interest payment is not only defensible but in every sense desirable, but in so doing they are going beyond the sphere of commercial banking, which alone is under consideration at this point.

Rates charged on loans and discounts are the chief means through which commercial banks are remunerated for the services they perform. In the long run these rates are determined by competition, and represent the current market value of the services performed by bankers. Custom often affects them temporarily and sometimes for long periods prevents their response to influences tending to produce change, but in the long run they yield to economic force and conform to the laws of value.

Variations in the rate of discount are the most efficient means employed by commercial banks for the regulation of the volume of their loans and discounts and for changing the percentage their reserves bear to deposits and note issues. An increase of these rates tends to check loans and discounts, to decrease deposits and note issues, to increase reserves, and consequently to raise the percentage of reserves to deposits and issues.

It checks loans and discounts by increasing the expense of conducting business operations on a credit basis, thus diminishing profits and sometimes causing losses, checking enterprise and decreasing the volume of commercial transactions. A decrease of loans and discounts correspondingly diminishes deposits or note issues, or both, since these are simply the counterpart or representative of such loans and discounts in the form of credit balances in the checking accounts conducted by the banks or the equivalent of such balances in a hand-to-hand money form. An increase in the rate of discount at a given point tends to attract funds from other points where the rates are lower and thus to increase reserves. A decrease of rates produces opposite effects all along the line.

4. Protection against Unsound Practices

Commercial banks are an essential part of the machinery by which the agriculture, industry, and commerce of a country are carried on, and their proper conduct is, therefore, a matter of public concern. On this account they have long been subjects of legislation and of public supervision and control. The methods evolved for safeguarding the public against abuses and unsound practices differ considerably among different nations and to some extent among the different states of the United States, and could only be adequately explained by a history of banking in each nation. Only the more important and most widely used of them will be described here.

(*a*) *Capital and Surplus Requirements and Double Liability of Stockholders.*—A very common, indeed, almost universal, legal requirement is that before beginning business the proprietors of a commercial bank shall contribute a fund to be known as the *capital stock*, and that an additional fund, usually called the *surplus*, shall afterwards be set aside from profits. These funds are required to be maintained intact, so long as the bank continues in business, and to be used for the payment of losses in case of failure or liquidation for any reason. In this country it is also customary to hold the proprietors legally liable in case of failure for an assessment equal to the amount of their capital stock. In foreign countries it is a common practice to have the subscribed considerably in excess of the paid-in capital, the balance being subject to call by the directors at any time, and being available for the payment of losses in case of failure.

These funds serve not only as a protection against loss to the customers of a bank in case of failure, but also as a restraining influence on the managers in the everyday conduct of the bank's affairs. They constitute the proprietors' stake in the business, what they are likely to lose if the management is imprudent, dishonest, or inefficient. The absence of such funds would put a premium on rashness and speculation and tempt into the business the unscrupulous and the unfit.

In the determination of the size of capital and surplus funds and of the amount of the liability of stockholders for subscriptions in case of failure, no well-founded principles have been developed for the guidance of legislators. They should be great enough to cover prospective losses and to induce conservatism, honesty, and efficiency in management, and not so great as to prevent the free flow of an adequate amount of capital into the business. Unfortunately, the statistics of losses in cases of failure are not a sufficient guide. In some cases they bear a large proportion to the volume of business transacted and in others a very small one, and the number of cases available are too small to give much value to averages. The amount necessary to secure the best possible management is also purely problematical.

In lieu of well-founded principles, the practice has developed in this country of making the minimum capitalization permitted depend upon the population of the town in which the bank is located. This seems to be a very crude and indirect method of proportioning capital to the volume of business transacted. The fixing of such a proportion, or of a proportion which no bank should be permitted to exceed, is probably the best method of solving this problem, but it should be done directly and not by the roundabout method which has been mentioned above.

A proportion of ten to one between capital and aggregate demand obligations would probably be justified by American experience. The present practice of fixing the surplus fund at twenty per cent of the capital would be justifiable if the capital fund were properly regulated in amount.

(b) *Inflation and Means of Protecting the Public against It.*—The greatest abuse to which the business of commercial banking is subject, and against which the public most needs protection, is inflation. This is a condition difficult to diagnose, and not well understood by the general public and even by bankers. The most easily recognized symptom of its existence is the forced liquidation of credits; that is, forced sales of property in order to meet maturing obligations to banks. When, for example, the people whose notes or bills have been discounted by banks default in large numbers, and the collateral deposited as security has to be sold, or, in the absence of collateral, the courts must order the sale of their property, the presence of inflation may be suspected.

28

The chief cause of inflation is the issue by commercial banks of demand obligations against investment securities. The means of liquidating such securities are the profits of the enterprises in which the investments were made and in the nature of the case several years are required for the accomplishment of this end. Meantime the demand obligations of the banks issued against them in the form of balances on checking accounts or notes must be met and, the funds regularly deposited with them as a result of the operation of such enterprises being inadequate, other means must be found. The only one available is the sacrifice, at forced sales, of the property in which the investment was made or of some other property in the possession of the persons responsible to the bank.

The banks usually protect themselves against such forced liquidation by the requirement that the paper they discount shall mature at short intervals, usually not to exceed four to six months, and accept the long-time securities, such as bonds, stocks, and mortgages, only as collateral. By this means they are able to force the liquidation on their customers. Otherwise they would be obliged themselves to endure it, with the result that their capital and surplus funds would be impaired and perhaps exhausted; and, if they should prove inadequate, failure would be inevitable.

The evil involved in the forced sales of property caused by inflation is the readjustment of prices through which it is accomplished, and the depression and, sometimes, panic which follow. When the prices of many kinds of property must be greatly depressed in order to induce their transfer to other hands, the machinery of commerce and industry is thrown out of adjustment and is sometimes rendered temporarily useless. This result is due to the fact that the relations between costs of production and the returns from the sale of finished products are so changed that profits are reduced or annihilated, and many persons are financially ruined. Readjustments of the prices of raw products, labor, and finished goods, and the transfer of plants to new hands, are, therefore, necessary before industry, commerce, and agriculture can again operate in a normal way, and during the period of readjustment some enterprises must entirely stop operations, and all must slow down. At such times many laborers are thrown out of employment, many more work part time only, the wages of nearly all are lowered, and most other classes of income are cut down. Depression and, in extreme cases, panic are the result, and these have serious consequences other than financial.

The means employed for the protection of the public against inflation are crude and inadequate. They may be grouped under the heads: regulations regarding investments, reserves, and note issues. Under the first head belong in the banking legislation of this country limitations on real estate investments and on the amount that may be loaned to a single firm or individual. Our national banking act and most of our state banking acts prohibit banks from holding real estate except for their own accommodation, and as a means of reimbursing themselves for defaulted loans, and our national banking act prohibits the taking of real estate security for loans, and many of our state banking acts limit the amount of such security that may be held. Our national banking act limits the amount that may be loaned to a single firm or individual to one-tenth of the bank's capital and surplus, and similar regulations are common in state banking legislation.

The purpose of these regulations is to confine the investments of banks to what are called liquid securities, but they fail to evince a proper conception on the part of their authors of what really makes a security liquid. Apparently legislators and their advisers have felt that if the securities held by the banks mature in short periods, or are listed on a stock exchange, they are liquid; but such is not necessarily the case.

Commercial paper only is really liquid, since it represents a current commercial process which will soon be completed and the completion of which automatically provides the means for its payment. Such paper usually matures in short periods, but the characteristic of liquidity results not from the date at which it is made to mature, but from the commercial process which called it into existence and will ultimately retire it. In this country very often paper of short maturity is so in form only, its makers expecting to renew it, instead of pay it, at maturity.

Bonds and stocks, even though they may be listed on a stock exchange and daily bought and sold, are not liquid securities in the proper sense of that term. An individual bank may be able to sell them in case of need, but such sale is simply the transfer of the investment to another bank or person, and not its liquidation. The security still exists and must be paid,

30

while its liquidation would take it out of existence.

Foreign legislators have approximated more closely than ours what is needed in the regulation of bank investments. In the case of their central banks, many of them, notably those of France and Germany, have recognized the fundamental distinction between commercial and investment paper, and have required them to hold the former against their demand obligations, especially their notes.

The regulation of reserves has become a subject of legislation in this country only. Our national banking act classifies national banks into three groups, called country, reserve city, and central reserve city banks, and requires those in the first mentioned group to keep cash in their vaults to the amount of at least six per cent of their deposits, and balances in approved reserve city banks sufficient to bring the total amount up to fifteen per cent of their deposits.

Banks in reserve cities are required to keep in their vaults cash to the amount of at least twelve and one-half per cent of their deposits, and balances in central reserve cities sufficient to bring the total up to twenty-five per cent of their deposits. Banks in central reserve cities are required to keep at least twenty-five per cent of their deposits in cash in their vaults. When the reserves of a bank fall to the prescribed minimum, all discounting must cease. Regulations essentially similar are found in the banking laws of most of our states.

The purpose of these regulations is to set a limit to the extent to which banks may expand the volume of their loans and discounts, in the belief, apparently, that, if at least the prescribed proportion of cash is all the time kept on hand, the banks will be able to meet their obligations. As in the case of the regulations concerning investments, the authors of these failed to recognize the significance, from the point of view of the cash demands likely to be made upon banks, of the kind of paper admitted to discount. If discounts be confined to commercial paper, the demand obligations they create will be met for the most part by transfers of credits on the banks' books or by the return of the notes issued, and, as foreign experience has demonstrated, the adjustment of cash resources to needs can safely be left to the judgment of the bankers themselves, who, through variations in the discount rate, rediscounts, and other means, can regulate it with ease. If investment paper is admitted to discount, reserves less than one hundred per cent of the demand obligations thereby created are unsafe, since a less amount is likely to force liquidation on the banks' customers, with the results above indicated.

The most elaborate regulations for the prevention of inflation have been developed in connection with legislation concerning note issues. The reason for this is the fact that commercial banking was at its origin and for a long time thereafter carried on almost exclusively through note issues, the conduct of checking accounts being a comparatively recent development. The phenomenon of inflation was, therefore, first observed in connection with note issues and associated with them. Even now the essential similarity of note issues and checking accounts as banking instrumentalities is not universally recognized.

The means of safeguarding note issues which have been incorporated into legislative enactments are the prior lien on assets, the safety fund, the requirement and sometimes the mortgaging of special assets, and the limitation of the total issues. By the prior lien is meant the provision that in case of failure the note holders shall be paid in full before any of the assets are distributed among other creditors. By the safety fund is meant a required contribution from each bank, usually a percentage of the amount of notes issued, placed in the hands of some public official and kept for the redemption, in case of failure, of such of the notes of failed banks as cannot be redeemed out of the assets of the banks themselves. Additional contributions from the solvent banks are required for the replenishment of the fund when it has been depleted.

The practice of different countries regarding the requirement of special assets to be held against note issues, as well as regarding the mortgaging of such assets, is not the same. Germany and France, for example, require their banks to cover their note issues by designated proportions of commercial paper and coin, while the United States requires its banks of issue to cover their notes by government bonds and to contribute a five per cent redemption fund in addition, and England requires the Bank of England to cover a designated amount of its issues by

32

government and other securities and the remainder by coin. Unlike the others, the United States mortgages to the note holders the securities, that is, the government bonds, required to be held against the notes, by providing that in case of failure these securities shall be sold and the proceeds used for the settlement of their claims.

In all of these provisions, the protection of note holders against loss in case of failure has been an influential consideration, and in the cases of the prior lien and the safety fund, the only one. The prevention of inflation may have entered into consideration in the other cases, but among the states mentioned the regulations of France and Germany alone are efficient in this direction, since they alone prohibit note issues against investment securities. The above mentioned regulations of England and the United States tend rather to promote, than to prevent, inflation, since they require the holding of investment securities against note issues.

The limitation of the aggregate amount of notes that may be issued is a common legislative regulation. In the United States the limit set is the amount of the capital stock, and in France it is an arbitrary figure from time to time changed as the needs of the bank seem to require. As a safeguard against inflation, the value of such limitation depends upon the basis of the issues. If it is investment securities, as in the case of the United States, limitation to a low figure, not in any case to exceed the capital stock, is desirable, since such limitation keeps the inflation within such bounds that the banks themselves may be able to withstand the effects of it by selling upon foreign markets, without great and perhaps without any loss, the securities in which their capital and surplus funds are invested. If the basis of issues be commercial paper, such limitation is unnecessary, since inflation in such a case is improbable, and pernicious, unless it be placed above the point which the volume of issues is likely in ordinary cases to reach.

(*c*) *Other Means of Safeguarding the Interests of the Public.*—Experience has shown that publicity is a valuable safeguard against bad bank practices, and legislation has, therefore, provided for it by the requirement that statements of banking operations shall be published from time to time. The national banking act of the United States and many of our state banking acts, for example, provide for the publication five times a year of bank balance sheets, drawn up according to prescribed forms.

The inspection of banks by public examiners and the requirement of detailed reports to public officials are also provided for in our federal and state legislation. Canada requires the reports but not the inspection by public officials, on the ground that the latter cannot be thorough and efficient, and is, therefore, likely to mislead the public and cause it to be less vigilant than it otherwise would be in the use of other means of safeguarding its interests.

Legislation in this country has also concerned itself with the duties of bank directors and the enforcement of their performance, and with the relations of bank officers to their banks, particularly those involved in borrowing for their own uses or for firms or corporations in which they are interested.

A recent legislative experiment along quite a new line has been undertaken in this country in the form of laws providing for the mutual insurance of depositors. Oklahoma started this experiment, and her example has been followed by other states. The essence of the experiment consists in the provision of a fund out of which is paid to the depositors of failed banks that portion of their claims which cannot be met from the liquidation of the assets of the defunct banks, such fund to be contributed by the other banks belonging to the system.

The protection of depositors against loss is a commendable aim of legislation, but this method of attaining this aim is open to the serious objection that it removes from depositors all concern regarding the proper management of the bank with which they do business, and thus gives the unscrupulous, dishonest, and plunging banker an advantage. Attraction of depositors is the chief field in which competition between banks is carried on, and when the power of good management in this direction is removed, high rates on deposits, high lines of credit, low or no rates of exchange, extravagance in equipment, etc., remain the only attractions, and in the offer of these the unscrupulous and plunging banker will always outdo the conservative.

It is impossible to overcome this objection by public supervision, and more frequent and rigid examinations. No public officer can equip himself to pass judgment on the relations of a bank with each customer, or to detect secret contracts and unwritten understandings, or to keep unscrupulous people out of the banking business. There can be no doubt that a reputation for conservatism, good judgment, strict integrity, and careful management is, at the present time, the most valuable asset a banker can have, because customers know that they are in danger to the extent that these qualities are lacking. To substitute for the present basis of competition between banks that established by mutual insurance laws is to undermine the foundations of our credit system and to invite disaster and ruin.

5. Adequacy and Economy of Service

From the point of view of adequacy and economy of service, two types of banking systems require attention; namely, that characterized by a large number of relatively small local independent banks, chartered under general laws, and exemplified in this country; and that characterized by a relatively small number of large banks endowed with the privilege of establishing branches, and exemplified in the other leading nations of the world.

Under our system each community is encouraged to look after its own banking needs. Local initiative in the establishment of new institutions is given free play and local capital and local talent is attracted. Outside promoters and outside capital are not excluded, but, if they come, they do so as colonists expecting to cast in their lot with the community and to become identified with it. The managers of our banks for the most part are local men who are the real heads of the institutions they manage and whose careers and prosperity depend on the success of these institutions.

The localism which characterizes this system contributes elements both of strength and of weakness. It develops local talent, and promotes mutual understanding and cooperation between the banks and the business enterprises of the community, and conformity of organization and methods to local needs. Its weakness consists in the financial isolation and the narrowness of vision and training which are its natural accompaniments. Under this system capital does not easily and quickly move from place to place and readily distribute itself according to the relative needs of different communities. In consequence, rates of interest are apt to vary widely, some communities to be under- and others over-capitalized, and the capital of the nation as a whole to be inefficiently employed. Under this system the opportunity of bankers for training is meager, since the broader and more fundamental aspects of the business are rarely brought to their attention, and in the smaller towns and country districts they are apt to be recruited from people of mediocre ability and often from those not well fitted by nature and education for this branch of commercial enterprise.

The system of branch banking, almost universally employed elsewhere, is strong where our system is weak, but it has weaknesses of its own. It promotes distribution of capital according to relative needs, and consequently efficiency in the application of a nation's capital as a whole, and it offers a wide field of training for the people engaged in the business, and draws its recruits from every quarter. It can readily supply banking facilities to communities too small or too poor to provide for an independent bank, and more readily than our system can adjust itself to rapidly growing communities.

Its chief weakness consists in the lack of independence of the managers of the branches and the consequent danger that local needs may not be fully satisfied. The manager of a branch is usually granted freedom of action only in routine matters. Any business out of the usual order must be referred to higher authorities connected or associated with the main office; and, even with the advice of the manager, who alone is familiar with local conditions, the decision cannot be made with that intimacy of knowledge of and sympathy with the business and aspirations of the individual or firm under consideration that full justice to him and his town may require. In the matter of adequacy and character of service, therefore, the city in which the main office is located has an advantage over those in which the branches are located.

In this connection it should also be noted that, while the branch banking system is able to adjust itself to the capital requirements of towns of all sizes more readily than the independent banking system, and thus to secure a better distribution of the banking capital of the community, it does not follow that it will do so. On account of ignorance of conditions, insufficiency of capital or inability readily to increase it, or inertia on the part of the head office, a town may have to wait for the establishment of a branch longer than it would for the establishment of an independent bank.

Whether or not this will be the case, however, depends to a considerable extent upon the keenness of the competition between the big banks with branches. The big central banks of Europe, which have no competition within their field, have been slow to establish branches. The coercive force of the government has been necessary in many cases to secure their proper expansion. In the case of the other big banks, however, both of Europe and of Canada, competition has resulted in very rapid expansion during the last half century, probably as rapid as could be desired.

Regarding adequacy of service, the method of granting charters and the attitude of the government towards private banking is important. If banks are allowed to spring up spontaneously, like manufacturing and commercial establishments and farms, they are likely to be plentiful and to be located wherever needed. Experience, however, has shown that private banks cannot be adequately regulated in the interest of the public and that incorporation under public auspices should be required.

Two methods of incorporation are employed, those of the special charter and of the general law. Except in the case of special institutions, like central banks, the former is objectionable, since it opens the doors to political favoritism and is likely to result in bad distribution, lack of uniformity in regulation, and lack of steadiness and regularity in development. Incorporation under general laws, or the free banking system, as it is sometimes called in this country, is unquestionably the best from every standpoint. All the necessary checks and balances can be incorporated in these laws, and the supervision of public officers, together with the necessary administrative machinery, provided for. This is the only practicable method to employ in an independent system like ours.

The special charter method works best in connection with the branch bank system, in which the question of chartering new institutions only occasionally arises, and in which delay is not so serious.

CHAPTER IV

Commercial Banking in the United States

The commercial banking system of the United States consists of several elements which have been contributed at different periods in our history. The most important of these are state banks, national banks, and the independent treasury system.

1. State Banks

From the very beginning of our national history institutions enjoying, among others, the privilege of commercial banking have been chartered by our states. For several years after the adoption of our constitution it remained an open question whether the incorporation of such institutions was not their exclusive privilege, but in the case of McCulloch v. Maryland, in 1819, the Supreme Court decided that the federal government also had this right.

During the years 1791-1811, and 1816-1836, the state banks had as competitors the first and second United States banks, and in 1863 so-called national banks entered the field, and, more recently still, trust companies. Private banks have also existed from the beginning, but their number and relative importance have declined in recent years. At the present time the number of state banks exceeds that of all other classes of banking institutions combined, but in capital and resources they are inferior to both national banks and trust companies.

Since each state has had a free hand in the matter of legislation concerning the banks chartered under its auspices, uniformity in the regulations imposed upon and in the kind and degree of supervision exercised over this class of institutions, is lacking. In most cases, however, as compared to national banks, the amount of capital required is smaller; they have greater freedom in the making of loans, especially upon real estate security; and they are not so carefully examined and supervised by public officials. The most frequently imposed legislative requirements are: the accumulation of a surplus fund from earnings; double liability of stockholders; a minimum cash reserve to be kept in the vaults, and an additional reserve on deposit in other banks; the organization of a banking department for the administration of the laws pertaining to them; regular reports and examinations; and some limitation on real estate holdings and on the amount of loans to be made on real estate security. On account of the relatively low capital requirements imposed upon them, and the liberality of the laws concerning them in other respects, state banks have been able to prosper where national banks and trust companies could not exist, and on this account in many parts of the South and West they do most of the banking business in small towns and country districts. They generally perform a wide range of banking functions, including those of investment and savings as well as of commercial banks.

2. *National Banks*

Our national banking system owes its existence to financial exigencies of the federal government experienced during the Civil War. For a considerable period preceding the outbreak of that struggle the expenses of the government had exceeded its receipts. The deficit was greatly increased as soon as the war began, and Congress did not find it possible immediately to devise adequate new sources of revenue, including a market for government bonds. It was, therefore, forced to the issue of legal-tender notes under authority of an act passed February 25, 1862.

After three issues of these notes, amounting to $400,000,000, had been exhausted, and the value of the notes had depreciated to such an extent that persistence in this method of financiering portended speedy financial disaster, Congress adopted a suggestion made early in the war by Secretary Chase, to the effect that a market for government bonds might be created by compelling banks to purchase them as security for their note issues. An act passed February 25, 1863, provided for the incorporation of banks with the right to issue notes on condition that they purchase government bonds and deposit them with an official to be known as Comptroller of the Currency.

It was the expectation of the authors of this act that the state banks, then numbering over one thousand, would exchange their state for national charters and purchase bonds sufficient to secure their circulation under the terms of the new act, but, since they showed reluctance so to do, in 1865 force was applied in the form of a tax of ten per cent on bank notes otherwise secured. Under this pressure most of the state banks reorganized as national institutions, but a few retained their state charters and formed the nucleus of the state system of the present day. On account of the ten per cent tax, however, the issue of notes by this remnant became unprofitable, and the new national banks have to this day remained the sole banks of issue in the country.

The act of 1863 has been amended several times, notably in 1864, 1870, 1874, 1875, 1882, 1887, and 1900. In its present form it permits the organization of banks with a capitalization as low as $25,000 in towns of 3,000 inhabitants or less, and with a capitalization as low as $50,000 in towns of 6,000 or less. Banks organized under this act must put ten per cent of their profits into a surplus fund until said fund amounts to twenty per cent of the capital; must invest at least twenty-five per cent of their capital, if it is less than $200,000, and at least $50,000, if it is $200,000 or more, in government bonds; and may deposit said bonds with the Comptroller of the Currency and receive circulating notes to the amount of their par value, provided their market value is par or above.

The rights and privileges of these banks are stated in very broad and general terms, a fair interpretation of which permits them to engage in both commercial and investment banking under certain specified limitations, of which the most important are the following: they must not invest in or hold real estate beyond their owns needs for suitable quarters, or temporarily for the purpose of collecting debts due them; they must not accept real estate as security for loans; they must not loan more than ten per cent of their capital and surplus to any one person or firm; and they must keep reserves to the amount of fifteen per cent of their deposits, if they belong to the group known as country banks, and to the amount of twenty-five per cent of their deposits, if they belong to either the reserve city or the central reserve city group.

In the case of country banks, at least two-fifths of the required reserves, and in the case of reserve city banks, at least one-half, must consist of specified forms of money in their own vaults. The remainder may be balances payable on demand in approved banks in reserve or central reserve cities in the case of country banks, and in the central reserve cities in the case of reserve city banks. In the case of banks in central reserve cities, the entire reserve prescribed by law must consist of money in the vaults. These required minimum reserves must not be infringed upon. When a bank's cash and balances with its reserve agents fall to the prescribed minimum, discounting must be stopped under penalty of suspension of privileges and liquidation by the Comptroller of the Currency.

At five dates each year, selected by the Comptroller of the Currency, national banks must make detailed reports of their condition on prescribed blanks and publish abstracts of such reports in local newspapers. They must also submit to examination by persons appointed for that purpose by the Comptroller as often as this official may deem necessary and proper.

National banks have been organized in every state of the Union, and in Maine, Massachusetts, and Vermont they have completely supplanted the state banks. Elsewhere they exist side by side with state banks and compete with them. In some states they are more and in others less numerous than state banks. In the kind of business transacted the only important difference between the two classes of institutions consists in the loans on real estate security, which national banks are prohibited, and state banks allowed, to make. The latter, therefore, share this class of business with the trust companies only, and where it predominates have a distinct advantage in competition over the national institutions.

3. The Independent Treasury System

While not a banking institution, the Treasury of the United States handles its funds in such a manner and performs such functions with reference to the currency that it has become an important part of the banking system of the country.

Previous to 1840 the funds of the federal government were kept on deposit in banking institutions, during the greater part of the time in the First and Second United States banks. Friction between President Jackson and the Second United States Bank resulted in their withdrawal from that institution in 1834 and their deposit in selected state banks, several of which failed and all of which suspended specie payments during the crisis of 1837. The embarrassment which the treasury experienced in consequence, combined with previous unsatisfactory relations between the government and its depositories, convinced President Van Buren that the Treasurer ought himself to keep and to disburse the funds of the government. He made a recommendation to this effect to Congress, which in accordance therewith enacted the first independent treasury act in 1840. The revival of agitation for a third United States Bank led to the repeal of this act the following year, but in 1846 it was reenacted and with modifications has remained upon our statute books to the present day.

In its original form this act provided for the acquisition of vaults in certain cities, in which should be deposited the funds of the government as soon as possible after they came into the hands of the receiving officers, and out of which should be taken, upon drafts issued by the Secretary of the Treasury, the money needed for the payment of the government's obligations. It further provided that all dues to the government in the future should be paid either in coin or in currency issued exclusively by the government, and that all expenses should be paid in the same forms of money.

Important modifications in this act were made during and after the Civil War. In 1863 permission was granted the Secretary of the Treasury to deposit in national banks funds accumulated in the treasury, and derived from any source except duties on imports, provided the banks selected for this purpose should deposit with him government bonds for their security. Subsequently the discretionary power of the Secretary in this direction was extended so that at the present time he is authorized at his discretion to deposit in national banks surplus funds derived from any source, trust funds alone excepted, and to accept as security therefor other securities than government bonds. Other laws have made national bank notes acceptable for certain public dues, and have given the Secretary authority to issue gold and silver certificates against gold coin and silver dollars deposited in corresponding amounts, and to redeem United States notes in gold coin and to keep on hand for that purpose a gold reserve of $150,000,000.

In its operation, this independent treasury system affects the reserves of the banks and through them their discounts and the commerce of the country. Whenever the receipts of the government exceed its expenditures, money accumulates in the treasury and the reserves of the banks are diminished; and, under opposite conditions, they are increased. The return of accumulated surplus funds to the banks is possible when the Secretary of the Treasury decides that such return is desirable or necessary and when the banks are able and willing to supply the bonds demanded as security. In case a deposit is agreed upon the funds go to a relatively small number of national banks selected as depositories by the Secretary of the Treasury, the amount allowed each depository also being determined by him.

Through its ability to issue gold and silver certificates, its obligation to redeem United States notes in gold on demand, its administration of the United States mints and assay offices and the laws regulating the supply and distribution of subsidiary coin, the United States Treasury cooperates with the banks in the supply and distribution of the circulating medium of the country. The people apply to the banks for the forms of money and currency desired and these institutions meet the demand by means of the funds deposited with them or by their exchange at the various subtreasuries, if the forms of money deposited do not correspond with these demands.

4. The Interrelations of These Institutions

Under the operation of the national banking act, New York, Chicago, and St. Louis have been designated as *central reserve*, and forty-seven other cities as *reserve* cities. The national banks in these reserve cities act as reserve agents for national banks in the cities and towns not so designated and ordinarily receive on deposit the major part of their reserves plus surplus funds not needed for local purposes. Banks in the central reserve cities act as reserve agents for the banks in the reserve cities as well as for country banks, and on account of their importance as commercial and investment centers receive and hold in the form of bankers' balances a large part of the reserve funds as well as the surplus investment funds of the national banks of the entire country.

State banks and trust companies manage their reserve and surplus investment funds in substantially the same manner as national banks, using national banks in the reserve and central reserve cities as their reserve agents. State laws usually allow approved state banks and trust companies also to act as reserve agents for the banks and trust companies under their jurisdiction, but these approved banks are generally located in the reserve and central reserve cities, and themselves employ the national banks there located as their reserve agents, thus forming simply an additional conduit through which the reserve and surplus investment funds of state banks and trust companies reach the central money reservoirs administered by national banks in the central reserve cities.

National banks in the reserve and central reserve cities are also clearing centers for the enormous volume of checks and drafts which the administration of the checking accounts of the banks and trust companies of the country bring into existence. They act as correspondents as well as reserve agents for these other banks and trust companies, and in this capacity collect out-of-town checks and drafts and conduct checking accounts for them. Within these cities, as well as in hundreds of others, clearing house associations conduct the local clearings and also act as agencies through which national and state banks and trust companies cooperate in the promotion of common interests.

The center of the entire system is in New York City. The clearing house association of that city, consisting of over fifty national and state banks and trust companies, includes the banks the vaults of which constitute the central money reservoir of the country and which constitute the center of the country's clearing system. Through the New York subtreasury pass the greater part of the receipts and disbursements of the government, and the chief assay office in the country is located there. The New York stock exchange is our only stock and bond market of national scope, and consequently the investment center of the country.

The Associated Banks of New York City, as the members of the clearing house association are called, hold the greater part of the reserves of the banks and trust companies not required by law to be kept in the local vaults, as well as the greater part of the surplus investment funds of the entire country. It is through the operation of the New York subtreasury on the reserves of the Associated Banks that the chief influence of the independent treasury system on the banking business of the country is exerted, the greater part of the government's receipts coming directly out of those reserves, and a large part of the expenditures going into them, and the greater part of the money deposited in national banks by the Secretary of the Treasury going directly or indirectly into New York institutions. Most of the exports and imports of coin and bullion pass through New York, and the major portion of the foreign exchanges of the entire country are there effected. The New York Assay Office receives and distributes the greater part of the new supplies of gold and silver bullion which come from our mines and transforms into bullion the major part of these metals that come to us from abroad and do not find employment as foreign coin. The New York Stock Exchange is the medium through which a large part of the surplus savings of the country are invested in our industries or loaned for the use of our national, state, municipal, and other local governmental agencies.

5. Operation of the System

The most noteworthy features of the working of this machinery may be discussed under the heads: conflict of functions and laws; loan operations; treasury operations; reserve system; absence of elasticity in the currency.

(a) *Conflict of Functions and Laws.*—The two classes of banking institutions which have been described (state banks and national banks) and trust companies, described in a subsequent chapter, exist side by side in many communities, and in the performance of certain services compete for the patronage of the public. As has already been pointed out, state and national

45

banks differ little in their functions except in their relation to real estate loans, and in some states trust companies perform all the functions of these institutions and many others besides. In the performance of these common services, however, they are rarely regulated by the same laws or subjected to the same kind or degree of public supervision. The competition between them, therefore, is not always on a fair basis and the temptation to violate restraining laws and administrative regulations is strong. The supervising officers recognize the situation as a rule and go to the extreme limit of leniency in administering laws and regulations which operate to the manifest disadvantage of the institutions over which they have jurisdiction, but even then it is often impossible to render the basis of competition fair and equitable.

This condition of affairs has resulted in the devising of ways and means of circumventing obnoxious laws and in some cases in practices which are pernicious in themselves. As examples may be mentioned the widespread practice of national banks, which are prohibited by law from making loans on real estate security, of making loans to customers who can offer no other collateral, on the security of their personal notes only, or of making loans secured by real estate by a three cornered operation utilizing a director or officer or some other third party as intermediary. All three classes of institutions compete in soliciting the savings deposits of the community, with the result that the trust companies and savings banks, which often have the advantage here, sometimes force upon their state and national bank competitors a higher rate of interest on such deposits than they ought to pay. The differing regulations in some places in force regarding the amount that may be loaned to a single individual or firm has also resulted in some cases in devious and uncommendable practices.

For the remedy of these conditions the first desideratum is the careful differentiation of the various functions performed by all these institutions, and the devising of appropriate legal and administrative regulations for each one. These regulations should then be incorporated into the legislation and the administrative practices of the federal government and of each state, and any institution which performs any of these functions should be obliged to submit to the regulations pertaining thereto. The difficulties in the way of securing such a differentiation of functions and such community of action between the federal government and our states are too obvious to require statement, but they should not prevent the formulation of ideal conditions, and a conscious and persistent effort to attain them.

(*b*) *Loan Operations.*—In making loans, a typical method of procedure for a business man is to arrange with a bank for what is technically called a "line," that is, the maximum amount he may expect to be able to borrow under normal conditions. This "line" determined, he borrows from time to time according to his needs, giving as security his personal note, payable in one, two, three, four, or six months. Sometimes an indorser is required, and sometimes the deposit of collateral, mortgages on real estate, bonds, stocks, and warehouse receipts being the most commonly used securities employed in such cases. Ordinarily, when a note falls due, he expects the bank to renew it, if its payment at the time is not convenient, the agreement on a "line of credit" ordinarily carrying with it that implication, though not legally, probably not morally, binding the bank so to do. Indeed, the customer ordinarily counts the amount of his "line" as a part of his working capital and expects to keep it in use a large part, if not all, of the time.

In the determination of the amount of these "lines of credit," the judgment of some one or more bank officers, assisted by a discount committee and sometimes, though not as a rule, by a specially organized credit department, rules. In forming these judgments, the bankers of the United States as a class are not guided by any universally recognized and well established principles. The best ones require from their customers carefully prepared statements showing the nature and volume of the business they transact, and a careful classification of their assets and liabilities. Others, and these are a large majority, rely upon the knowledge they already possess, gained by general observation, and supplemented by verbal inquiries made from time to time and by the voluntary statements of the customers themselves.

The significance of the distinction between commercial and investment operations in the business of banking is not generally understood, and is consequently little regarded. The dominant question in the mind of the average banker, both in determining the amount of a customer's line and in making loans to him after the line is fixed, is how much he is "good for," and on this point the total net worth, rather than the nature of the business operations, of the customer is likely to be decisive. Of course, the banker is also influenced by the customer's reputation for both integrity and business ability.

This method of procedure has the advantage of rendering access of people to the banks easy and of promoting their extensive use, but it has the grave disadvantage of opening the doors wide to inflation of credit. The majority of our bankers do not know whether more or less than their savings deposits and their capital and surplus, the only funds which can safely be invested in fixed forms, is so invested. The promissory notes of their customers, which constitute the major part of their assets, give no information on this point, and they have not made the investigations necessary to determine with certainty the destination of the funds they have loaned. They are satisfied with the knowledge or the conviction that their loans can be collected, not at maturity—they know very well that many, probably most, of them can not—but ultimately. The result is that unconsciously and gradually the banks create their demand obligations in the form of balances on checking accounts against fixed investments in machinery, buildings, lands, mines, etc., and, when the payment of these obligations is demanded, the reserves fall below the danger point and they are forced to require payment at maturity of paper which the maker had counted upon having renewed indefinitely, and the payment of which is only possible by the forced sale of the property in which the borrowed funds were invested, or of some other property in his possession. If only a single bank or a comparatively few banks find themselves in this condition, relief may be found in the rediscount of paper with other banks, in direct loans, or in the sale of securities on the exchanges; but, if the condition is general, relief by these means is impossible, and widespread forced liquidation becomes necessary. An aggravated situation of this kind causes panic and results in a commercial crisis.

(c) *Treasury Operations.*—The operation of our independent treasury system produces arbitrary fluctuations in the reserves of the banks and prevents that degree of prevision which is essential to the most economical

48

and the safest practices. The funds needed for current purposes are withdrawn from the banks and kept under lock and key in the treasury vaults, thus diminishing reserves to the extent of their amount. Surplus funds likewise accumulate in the vaults with the same result, until the Secretary of the Treasury sees fit to deposit, and the banks find it possible to receive them. Even then the depository banks alone are directly benefited, and no one of these knows long in advance how much it is going to receive or when funds left on deposit will be withdrawn.

Since the volume of the business of the government is very large, the effects produced by the movement of its funds are of such magnitude as to give them national importance, the ability of banks to loan and to meet obligations already incurred being profoundly affected by them. Among these effects must also be noted the inability of the banks to calculate these movements in advance, as they to a degree can those produced by the operations of their commercial customers, and the relation between them and the Secretary of the Treasury, which results. The relation between the receipts and the disbursements of the government vary greatly from month to month and year to year, so that, on the basis of past experience, it is impossible to predict when the banks will gain from or lose to the treasury. The action of the Secretary of the Treasury regarding deposits of surplus funds is equally uncertain and unpredictable. No fixed policy regarding this matter has yet been established by precedent or determined by law. Each secretary follows his own judgment and is influenced by current events and conditions.

The uncertainty which results creates a speculative atmosphere about the money market and renders the banks dependent upon the secretary and the secretary influential on the money market in a manner which is unfortunate for both. Since they cannot be indifferent to the operations of the treasury, and cannot predict them, banks are obliged to speculate regarding them, and, if they err, they are likely either to over-extend their credit operations or unduly to contract them. The former will result when they expect an increase in their reserves from treasury sources and do not get it, and the latter when contemplated withdrawals of funds do not occur.

The Secretary of the Treasury is not in a position properly to exercise the power conferred upon him. He is outside the channels of commerce and industry, and must, therefore, secure at second hand the information necessary for intelligent action. Such sources of information are frequently unreliable and inaccurate and their use subjects him to the charge of favoritism and to the danger of acting in the interest of special groups or special localities.

(*d*) *Operation of the Reserve System.*—Each national bank now keeps locked up in its vaults money to the amount of at least six to twenty-five per cent of its deposits and a balance with banks in reserve and central reserve cities sufficient to bring the total to at least fifteen per cent of deposits in the case of country banks, and twenty-five per cent of deposits in the case of reserve city banks. In addition, it is customary for most banks to carry as a secondary reserve high-grade bonds which can be readily sold in case of need. The practice of state banks is practically the same as that of national, and that of trust companies differs only in the amount of reserves carried and in the proportion between the different items.

This system has many disadvantages. Among them the most obvious, perhaps, is the withdrawal of enormous sums from the current use of the agriculture, industry, and commerce of the country. That portion of these reserve funds which is required to be kept under lock and key in the vaults, amounting in the aggregate to a billion and a half of dollars or more, is not available for use in ordinary times, and is practically useless even in times of stringency, since according to present law, when the reserves fall to the minimum prescribed by law, banks must stop discounting, under penalty of being put in the hands of a receiver. The other portions of these funds, namely, those deposited with banks in reserve cities and those invested in bonds, are likewise withdrawn from the uses of current commerce, since a large part of the former is only available for use on the New York Stock Exchange, and the latter are invested in railroads, mines, factories, land, etc.

The explanation of the devotion of the redeposited portion of the reserves to the operations of the New York Stock Exchange is to be found in the fact that that exchange furnishes a regular market for call loans on a large scale. Since these funds are held subject to the call of the banks which deposited them, and interest at the rate of at least two per cent is paid upon them, the depository banks are bound to seek investment for them, and call

50

loans on collateral listed on the exchange under ordinary circumstances are best suited to their purposes.

Another disadvantage of this reserve system is the dangerous situation in which it places banks from time to time, and the tendency to panic which it fosters. The demands made upon banks for both cash and credit vary with the seasons. In the fall and spring they are much greater than in the winter and summer. They also vary regularly through periods of years, increasing during the up-grade of a credit cycle and decreasing for a longer or shorter period after a crisis. Irregular and unexpected events also cause variations. On account of the rigidity of this reserve system and the lack of elasticity in our currency, the means available to banks for meeting increased demands, especially those of an irregular and unexpected character, are inadequate, and their employment is often dangerous. These means are: keeping in the vaults in slack times a large amount of unused cash, a practice too expensive to be employed; keeping surplus balances with correspondents at two or three per cent interest, not a sufficiently remunerative practice to be employed on a sufficiently extensive scale; rediscount with correspondents of some of their customers' paper, or loans from them on the security of their own signatures or on such security supplemented by collateral; and sale of bonds at such prices as they will bring.

None of these expedients is certain at all times and under all conditions, and some of them are precarious at all times. Surplus balances with correspondents are most reliable, but they occasionally fail on account of the inability of correspondents to realize upon their call loans. When calls for the payment of balances are large and general, it is impossible for brokers whose loans are called by one bank to transfer them to another. The collateral deposited as security must, therefore, be offered for sale on the stock exchange, and the very stringency which resulted in their being so offered renders their sale, even at slaughter prices, difficult and sometimes impossible. The result at the best is a heavy fall in the prices of stock-market securities, and at the worst a stock-market panic and a suspension of payments by the banks.

Rediscounts and loans from correspondent banks cannot be depended on. Correspondents are under no obligation to make them. They will usually do so as a favor, if their condition warrants, otherwise not. Sales of bonds on the stock exchange are difficult and sometimes impossible in times of emergency, and are usually attended with loss.

On account of this uncertainty and the danger attending it, when new and unusual conditions likely to result in increased demands upon them arise, banks are likely to act "panicky"; to call in their balances from correspondents; to sell bonds; to call loans; and greatly to curtail or absolutely to cut off new discounts. This action spreads the panicky feeling among their customers, and creates such pressure at the reserve centers as to cause curtailment of accommodations and panic there.

At the very best, this reserve system is accompanied by high discount and loan rates and by speculation on the stock market. High rates result inevitably from the hoarding of currency which it involves, the supply of loan funds being abnormally diminished, and speculation follows from the concentration in slack times of funds in New York City, which can only be employed in call loans on stock-exchange collateral. Stock brokers regularly take advantage of this situation, speculate themselves and inspire speculation among their customers. The mutual dependence of the stock and money markets thus produced by this reserve system is disadvantageous to both, fluctuations in values, uncertainty, and irregularity on both being the result.

(e) *Lack of Elasticity in the Currency.*—The money of the United States consists of four main elements, gold and silver coin, United States notes, and national bank notes, and none of these fluctuate in volume in accord with the needs of commerce.

The gold element depends primarily upon the output of our gold mines and upon the international movement of gold, increasing when that output increases and when our imports of gold exceed our exports, and decreasing under opposite conditions. These fluctuations, however, are quite independent of our commercial needs. Silver dollars, which constitute the major part of our silver currency, for several years have been unchanged in quantity, and the volume of United States notes has remained at $346,681,016 since the resumption of specie payments, January 1, 1879.

National bank notes fluctuate in volume as a result of changes in the number of national banks and in the prices of government bonds. Whenever a new national bank is organized, a specified portion of its capital must be invested in government bonds, which bonds are usually deposited with the Comptroller of the Currency in exchange for notes; and, when the price of government bonds rises, banks holding more than the minimum required by law frequently retire a portion of their circulation in order to recover their bonds for sale at the enhanced price. When the price of government bonds falls, many banks purchase additional quantities and increase their circulation.

Changes in the price of government bonds and in the number of national banks, however, have no connection whatever with changes in our currency needs, and no more do the fluctuations in the volume of the currency as a whole, made up of these various elements combined. As a result of this condition, rates on loans and discounts fluctuate greatly on account of wide variations between the demand and the supply of loan funds, and commerce is hampered at certain seasons and overstimulated at others. As was indicated above, this lack of elasticity in our currency aggravates the defects of our reserve system and also aids in the production of financial panics.

6. Plans for Reform

On account of the defects in our system of banking, there has been long-continued agitation for reform, increasing in scope and intensity in recent years. After the crisis of 1907, which revealed these defects to many persons who had not observed them before, Congress appointed a commission to make investigations and to prepare a reform measure. In January, 1912, this committee submitted a report which embodied a bill for the incorporation of a National Reserve Association, to be made up of a federation of local associations of banks and trust companies. The purpose of this association was to supply a market for commercial paper, an elastic element in the currency, a place for the deposit of the bank reserves of the country and of the funds of the government, as well as proper machinery for the administration of this market and these funds.

For various reasons, the plan of the monetary commission did not meet with universal favor. It was condemned in particular by the Democratic party, which was victorious at the polls in the fall elections, and installed a new administration in Washington, March 4, 1913. A special session of the new Congress was called to consider the tariff question, and to it was submitted another plan for the reform of our banking system, which was enacted into law December 23, 1913.

This law provides for the incorporation of so-called "Federal Reserve Banks," the number to be not less than eight or more than twelve. The country is to be divided into as many districts as there are Federal Reserve Banks, and the national banks in each district must subscribe six per cent and pay in three per cent of their capital and surplus to the capital stock of the Federal Reserve Bank located in that district. State banks and trust companies may contribute on compliance with the same conditions as national institutions. If, in the judgment of the organization committee, the amount of stock thus subscribed is inadequate, the public may be asked to subscribe, and as a last resort stock sufficient to raise the total to an adequate figure may be sold to the Federal Government. Cooperation between these Federal Reserve Banks and a degree of unity in their administration are provided for through a Federal Reserve Board of seven members, two ex officio and five to be especially appointed by the President of the United States. For the administration of each Federal Reserve Bank, a board of directors of nine members is provided for, six to be appointed by the member banks and three by the Federal Reserve Board, one of those three to be designated as Federal Reserve Agent and to be the intermediary between the Federal Reserve Board and the bank of whose directorate he is a member.

The proposed Federal Reserve Banks are to hold a part of the reserves of member banks and to rediscount commercial paper, administer exchange accounts, and conduct clearings for them. They are also to serve as depositories for the United States government, and to issue treasury notes obtained from the Federal Reserve Board in exchange for rediscounted commercial bills, these notes to be redeemable on demand by them and to be a first lien on all their assets. Their retirement, when the need for them has passed, is provided for by the requirement that no Federal Reserve Bank shall pay out any notes except its own, all others being sent in to the issuing bank or to the treasury for redemption. Against outstanding note issues a reserve of at least 40 per cent in gold must be maintained, and against deposits one of at least 35 per cent in gold or lawful money.

This law provides remedies for the chief defects of our system; namely, a market for commercial paper which will enable a properly conducted bank at any time, through rediscounts, to secure notes, legal-tender money, or checking accounts in the amounts needed; a system of note issues which will fluctuate automatically with the needs of commerce for hand-to-hand money; a more economical administration of the reserve funds of the country, unattended by the dangers of the present system, and an administration of the funds of the federal government which is free from the evils of the independent treasury system.

CHAPTER V

Commercial Banking in Other Countries

In contrast with that of the United States, the characteristic features of the commercial banking systems of Europe are the central bank performing important functions for all other financial institutions and for the government; a relatively small number of large institutions with many branches mediating between the central bank and the people; and the use of commercial and bank bills instead of promissory notes as the chief instruments of loans and discounts.

1. Common Features

The central banks differ considerably in organization and business methods, but perform essentially the same functions; that is, they act as financial agents for their respective governments; discount high-grade commercial and bankers' bills for other banks and usually for private persons; administer the cash reserves of the entire country; and furnish the greater part and, in some cases, the entire supply of bank notes.

The other large banks do most of the business with the public, the central bank's relations being chiefly with them and with the government. They conduct checking accounts with merchants, manufacturers, farmers, and others; receive and invest savings deposits, and deal in certain classes of investment securities; conduct the domestic and foreign exchanges; discount various kinds of commercial and banking bills, frequently those not available for discount at the central bank; and make advances on personal and other kinds of security. Their main offices are located either in the central money market of the country or in important financial centers, and their branches are extended to all places in which banking facilities are supposed to be needed. As a rule, they are less restricted by legislative provisions than are the national and state banks and trust companies of the United States, and are less carefully supervised and inspected by public officers.

Commercial and bankers' bills are widely used as credit instruments between buyers and sellers and between bankers and their customers. A common method of procedure, when a sale is made on time, is the drawing of a bill for the amount due, by the seller upon the buyer, payable at the end of the credit period agreed upon, and accepted by the buyer, and the discount of the bill by the seller's bank. In foreign and in some branches of domestic trade, the banker's bill is used on account of its more general acceptability as an object of discount, such bills usually being discountable by the central bank and by banks far distant from the place in which the bill originated.

In case a buyer desires to furnish his creditors with bills of this kind, he arranges with his banker for a line of "acceptance" credit, which permits people who sell goods to him to draw bills upon his banker instead of himself, the banker agreeing to accept the bill and guaranteeing its payment at maturity. The seller will usually have no difficulty in discounting such a bill at his own bank, no matter how far removed it may be from the home of the buyer, the character of the accepting bank being known throughout the financial world. "Acceptance lines" are usually granted only on condition that the customer agrees to supply the bank with the funds necessary for meeting the accepted bills as they fall due, and to pay a fee for the accommodation. Ample security that these obligations will be met is usually demanded.

2. The English System

In the English system, the central bank is the Bank of England, with the possible exception of a few private banks, the oldest financial institution in the country. It is privately owned and privately governed. Its board of directors, chosen by the stockholders, consists of twenty-four persons, a portion of whom are practically life members, being regularly reelected when their terms of office expire. The others usually serve alternate years only, vacancies being filled by promising young men selected from the business houses of London. The oldest director is regularly elected to the office of governor of the Bank, and the next oldest to that of deputy governor, both serving two years, the deputy governor regularly succeeding to the office of governor, and the ex-governors forming the life members of the board and constituting a kind of advisory council to the governor, and known as the Board of Treasury.

The head office of the Bank of England is in London, and there are eleven branches, two in London and nine in the provinces. By a law passed in 1844, the Bank was divided into two departments, called respectively the banking and the issue departments, the latter having exclusive charge of the issue of notes, and the former of all other branches of the bank's business.

This same law prescribed the conditions under which notes could be issued. It provided that the Bank of England might issue £14,500,000 of notes in exchange for securities, and any amount in addition in exchange for an equal amount of coin or bullion. Additions to the amount issued in exchange for securities might be made by order of the government to the extent of two-thirds the amount of issues relinquished by the other issuing banks, all such banks in existence at the time the act was passed being permitted to retain, without increasing, their existing issues. Most of these other issues having been abandoned since 1844, the Bank of England is now permitted to issue in exchange for securities £18,450,000. The securities against which these issues are made were transferred to the issue department by the banking department, and consist of the debt owed by the government to the bank and of other government or governmentally guaranteed securities. The issue department freely issues additional notes in exchange for an equal amount of gold coin or bullion, and on demand redeems notes in gold coin. Since the amount of notes all the time outstanding greatly exceeds £18,450,000, the business of the issue department is confined to the exchange of notes for gold coin and bullion and the redemption of notes in gold.

The banking department receives and disburses the funds of the government, manages the public debt, and serves as the government's agent in most of its other financial operations; receives on deposit from other financial institutions the money which comes into their possession, and supplies them with such money funds as they need from day to day in payment of checks drawn against their balances; discounts bills of exchange with a minimum maturity of four, and in exceptional cases six, months; and to a limited extent makes advances on and invests in high-grade public and other securities. Besides the English government and financial institutions, it has other customers, but it is to be presumed that these are of a special character, since the conditions under which it does business with private persons are in most cases more onerous than those prescribed by other banks, and consequently not attractive to the ordinary business man.

The so-called English Joint-Stock Banks are classified into three groups, known as metropolitan, metropolitan and provincial, and provincial banks. The metropolitan banks have their head offices in London, and do not, as a rule, extend their branches beyond the suburbs of the metropolis. The metropolitan and provincial banks have their head offices in London and branches scattered throughout the provinces, as well as in various parts of the city and suburbs, and the provincial banks have their head offices in the larger provincial cities, and each one confines its branches usually to the town and country districts tributary to the city in which its head office is situated. Often the provincial banks establish branches in London.

For banking purposes, these banks are the chief reliance of the agriculture, industry, and commerce of the country, but competing with and supplementing them are the bill brokers and discount houses, the private banks, and the foreign and colonial banks. The bill brokers and discount houses make a business of dealing in foreign and domestic bills of exchange. They buy in the first instance a large percentage of the bills brought to market, keep some of them until maturity, and sell the remainder to the other banks, usually indorsing them first. A large part of the capital employed in their business is obtained by loans made from the other banks, subject to call and secured by the bills they purchase deposited as collateral.

The private banks are the remnant left of the oldest group in the country. There were private banks in London centuries before the Bank of England was incorporated, and previous to 1826 the Bank of England was their only competitor. Since 1844 their number has steadily diminished. Those which remain have, as a rule, built up a special constituency, to the special interests of which they cater. Among them are strong institutions, but as a class their importance in the system is not great, and is waning.

The foreign and colonial banks are branches of important institutions in foreign countries and the English colonies which have a considerable volume of business to transact in London. They serve as intermediaries between their respective countries and the English money market, and on account of the enormous volume of foreign commerce which is financed in London, their number is large, and the rôle they play on that market is important.

In the operation of this machinery, the most noteworthy features are the reserve system, and the administration of the discount rate of the Bank of England. There is no law on the English statute books prescribing the amount of cash which banking or other financial institutions shall keep in their vaults. The custom of these institutions regarding that matter is to keep on hand relatively small sums and to rely upon the Bank of England or some other London banking house for the replenishment of their supply as needed. For this purpose, London and many provincial banks keep balances with the Bank of England, and other banks maintain balances with other London institutions. These balances may be obtained by the deposit of coin or Bank of England notes or by rediscounts. Another widely used resource is the calling of loans made to bill brokers or discount houses. Such loans or a considerable volume of bills of the kind discounted by the Bank of England, or both, are regularly carried by London banks and counted as a part of their reserves.

On account of these practices, surplus cash not needed in the conduct of the current business of the country speedily finds its way into the vaults of the Bank of England, and additional supplies, when needed, come from this source. The administration of the cash reserves of the country thus becomes one of the important duties of the Bank of England, in the performance of which variation of the rate charged on discounts is the most important device.

Many years' experience has enabled the Bank to determine with a considerable degree of accuracy the volume of the demands for cash likely to be made upon it from day to day, and consequently the amount that it should keep on hand in the vaults. Whenever this amount approaches the minimum regarded as consistent with safety, the directors raise the rate of discount, and when the amount on hand becomes excessive, they lower it. The efficiency of this procedure in increasing the reserves in the one case and in decreasing them in the other is due to certain conditions and practices which deserve attention at this point.

Long-established custom has made the rate of interest paid on deposits in London and other parts of England vary with the discount rate of the Bank, and on this account the market rate of discount also varies in the same manner. The Bank of England is thus ordinarily able to regulate the market for commercial paper. Since paper payable in London is a favorite form of investment for continental bankers, by raising its rate of discount and with it the market rate above the level of the rates of some or all of the continental centers, the Bank of England is able to induce these bankers to send money to London for investment and thereby to increase her reserves, and by lowering its rate below the level of the rates in these continental centers, she is able to induce them to sell some of the paper they already hold, and thus to furnish a market for her surplus funds and diminish her reserves.

On account of the readiness with which the international gold movement responds to variations in the discount rate of the Bank of England, the need for an elastic system of bank note issues is not felt in England to the same extent as in other countries. It is this fact, doubtless, which explains the retention to the present day of the essentially inelastic bank note system created by the act of 1844.

3. The French System

In France, the Bank of France is the central institution. It is the oldest of the important French banks of the present day, having been established in 1800 by Napoleon the First. Its capital, amounting at the present time to 182,500,000 francs, or approximately $36,500,000, is supplied by about 30,000 private stockholders, about 10,000 of whom own only one share each.

The two hundred largest stockholders appoint a General Council, consisting of fifteen regents and three censors. Five regents and all the censors must be chosen from the commercial and industrial classes, and three of the remaining ten regents must be selected from the *tresoriers payeurs généreaux*, an important group of representatives of the public treasury scattered throughout the country. The General Council as well as the stockholders' assembly is presided over by a governor, who, together with two sub-governors, is appointed by the President of the Republic upon the nomination of the Minister of Finance. The governor is the chief executive officer of the bank and the final source of authority in most matters of vital importance. He is responsible to the government rather than to the stockholders, and is subject to removal only by the power which appointed him.

The Bank of France has about two hundred branches and sub-branches located in Paris and all the important cities and towns in the Republic, also over three hundred so-called agencies located in smaller places and transacting only a limited line of business. Each branch has a manager appointed in substantially the same manner as the governor, and the sub-branches and agencies are administered through the branches. Through this network of offices, every part of the country is brought into direct and easy access to the Bank.

The Bank of France is the only institution in the country privileged to issue circulating notes. The maximum allowed it is regulated by law and is increased from time to time. At present it amounts to 5,800,000,000 francs, or approximately $1,160,000,000. The bank is obliged to redeem these notes on demand in gold coin or silver five-franc pieces, but it is free to determine how much cash it shall keep on hand for that purpose, and when and under what conditions it shall issue them.

Its discount operations are limited by law to bills maturing in not more than three months, and bearing the signatures of at least three solvent persons, or two signatures and secured in addition by specified forms of collateral. It is also permitted to make loans or advances, as they are called, on securities of the French government maturing at fixed dates, gold and silver bullion, and the money of foreign countries, and obligations of the French railroads, French cities, and departments, the Crédit Foncier, and the Société Algerienne. It is also obliged to loan 180,000,000 francs ($36,000,000) to the government without interest.

One of the chief branches of the business of the Bank of France is the service of the public treasury and the performance of other financial duties imposed upon it by the government. It serves as the depository and disbursing agent for the government, and performs important functions connected with the public debt, the mints, the savings institutions, and publicly administered trusts of various kinds. It is also the depository for the banking reserves of the country. In France, as in England, it is not the custom of banking and other financial institutions to hoard money in their vaults, but to depend upon the Bank of France for supplies as needed. To this end they keep funds on deposit there, and regularly rediscount the paper of their customers when balances need to be replenished.

Through its network of branches and agencies spread over the entire country, the Bank of France is able economically and expeditiously to conduct the intermunicipal exchanges of the country. It participates in local clearings through membership in the clearing houses, at which balances are paid by checks drawn against credits on its books maintained for that purpose by all members, and it conducts so-called transfer accounts with other banks and financial institutions against which drafts can be drawn payable at any place where one of its offices is located. Such drafts constitute the chief means through which transfers of funds are made between different places.

The business of the Bank of France with private persons is limited by the requirement that all paper discounted must have three signatures, or two signatures and collateral security, and that advances can only be made on the security of the forms of collateral indicated above. Most business men find it either inconvenient or impossible to comply with these conditions, and consequently transact most of their business with other banking institutions. The third signature on paper discounted by the Bank is, therefore, usually supplied by these institutions, which thus act as an intermediary between the Bank and the commercial world.

Next to the Bank of France, the most important banking institutions of the country are the Crédit Foncier, the Crédit Lyonnais, the Comptoir d'Escompte de Paris, the Société Générale, and the Crédit Industrielle et Commercial. The Crédit Foncier is principally engaged in extending credit based on real estate security, but it also discounts large amounts of commercial paper. Its organization is modeled after that of the Bank of France, and, like that institution, it is controlled by the state. Since it is primarily an investment bank, a description of its principal operations will be deferred to the next chapter.

The four other banks mentioned are a product of the commercial life of modern France, all having been established since the revolution of 1848. They are all heavily capitalized, the smallest, the Crédit Industrielle et Commercial, having a capital of 100,000,000 francs ($20,000,000), and the largest, the Société Générale, having a capital of 400,000,000 francs

($80,000,000), and all extend their business by means of branches. The Crédit Lyonnais and the Comptoir d'Escompte have branches in France itself, the French colonies, and a number of foreign countries; the Société Générale, throughout France, in London, and San Sebastian, Spain; and the Crédit Industrielle et Commercial, in Paris and its suburbs. Taken together, these four institutions supply the French people in Paris and the Provinces with banking facilities for both their domestic and their foreign business. While in some of the larger provincial cities local banks with branches in surrounding towns and sometimes in Paris are to be found, branches of one or more of these four institutions are the chief reliance in nearly all places.

These institutions cater to all the financial needs of their constituents. They supply their needs for cash and for exchange; conduct checking accounts for them, although these are not used in France to the same extent as in the United States; discount their commercial paper and make loans to them on personal and other security; and receive on deposit their savings and provide them with investments. In performing these functions they make extensive use of the Bank of France and of the stock exchanges of the country. With the former they conduct checking and transfer accounts and rediscount their customers' bills, by these means procuring the coin, bank notes, and exchange needed; and from the latter they obtain the investment securities required for the satisfaction of both their own and their customers' needs.

Gold and silver coin and the notes of the Bank of France constitute the hand-to-hand money of the country. The latter form the elastic element, and their operation approximates perfection. When demand for money increases for any reason, more commercial bills are presented for discount to the banks, which, after indorsement, exchange them at the Bank of France for the notes with which they supply their customers' needs. The note issues of the Bank thus expand in direct and immediate response to the needs of the country for more currency. When such needs have passed, the discounted bills, in exchange for which these notes were issued, mature and are paid in greater volume than new bills are created and presented for discount, and notes, or a corresponding amount of coin, accumulate in the vaults of the Bank. The notes are cancelled and destroyed and the coin is kept in store until it again passes into circulation through exchange for notes still outstanding, or for discounted bills.

On account of the elasticity of its note issues, and the extent to which they are used in the commerce of the country, the Bank of France has occasion to change its rate of discount less frequently than any other bank in Europe. The result is that the country enjoys the advantage of steady and low rates, since in France, as in England, the discount rate of the central bank controls the market rate, and the ease and inexpensiveness with which the notes are issued make low rates possible.

4. The German System

The Imperial Bank, with head offices in Berlin, and about one hundred branches and more than four hundred sub-branches scattered throughout the country, plays essentially the same rôle in the German banking system that the Bank of England and the Bank of France play in the English and French systems, respectively. It was established in 1875 by an act which also profoundly affected the entire banking system of the country, and its development has been aided and directed by several acts passed subsequently.

Its capital, supplied by the general public, amounts at the present time to 180,000,000 marks ($45,000,000), and it is governed by three boards, known respectively as the Curatorium, the Direktorium, and the Central Ausschuss.

The Curatorium is composed of five members, of which body the Chancellor of the Empire is ex-officio chairman. A second member is appointed by the Emperor, and for that position he has always selected the Prussian Minister of Finance, and the three remaining members are appointed by the Bundesrath. It meets quarterly and reviews all the operations of the bank. It, or rather, the Chancellor, its chairman, has supreme power, which, however, he has never exercised except on one occasion, when he ordered the bank not to accept Russian securities as collateral for loans, an order since revoked.

The administration of the bank's affairs is chiefly in the hands of the Direktorium, consisting of a president, vice president, and seven other persons, all of whom are appointed by the Emperor for life, from a list of candidates recommended to him by the Bundesrath. This board selects the staff of bank officers and clerks, and superintends the daily conduct of the bank's business.

The Central Ausschuss is a committee of fifteen persons elected by and representing the stockholders. It holds monthly meetings; has the right to demand complete information concerning the bank's operations, to discuss all matters freely, and to tender advice and counsel; but it has no power to control except regarding two matters: it can set a limit to the amount of securities the bank can purchase, and can veto any proposed transactions with the Imperial Government or with the governments of any of the states.

Like the other central banks described above, it receives on deposit and disburses the funds of the Imperial Government; administers the coin reserves of the country; conducts the domestic exchanges, and serves as a bankers' bank. It is free to do business with the general public, but the legal and other limitations under which it must operate give the other banking institutions of the country the advantage in competition for this kind of business.

It shares the right of note issue with four other banks, which, out of thirty-two that retained that privilege at the time the Imperial banking system was established, alone retain it at the present time. The issues of these four institutions, however, are relatively small in volume, and the Imperial Government has the right to deprive them of it January 1, 1921, or any tenth year thereafter, on condition of giving one year's notice of its intention so to do. The issues of the Imperial Bank are subject to the following regulations: they must be covered by cash and discounted bills maturing in not more than three months, and signed by at least two solvent persons, the proportion of cash being not less than one-third of the total. If the total amount issued exceeds the Bank's holdings of gold bullion, specie, and government notes by more than 750,000,000 marks at the end of March, June, September, and December, and 555,000,000 marks at other times, a tax of five per cent per annum is levied on the excess.

The law confers upon the Bank the following powers:

a. To buy and sell gold and silver coin and bullion.

b. To discount, buy and sell bills of exchange whose maturity shall be three months at the longest, and for which usually three, and in no case less than two, accredited vouchers shall stand good; furthermore, to discount, buy and sell bonds of the Empire or of any German state, or domestic municipal corporations, provided such bonds mature within three months at the longest and conform to the new standards of value.

c. To grant interest-bearing loans for terms no longer than three months, upon movable security (lombard, or deposit loan business), such as: gold and silver, coined or uncoined; interest-bearing or non-transferable bonds maturing within a maximum term of three months, whether of the Empire, a German state, or of domestic municipal corporations; interest-bearing non-transferable bonds on which the interest is guaranteed by the Empire or by any one of the German states; capital stock and stock priority shares, fully paid up, of German railway companies in actual operation; mortgage bonds of the provincial, municipal, or other land credit institutions of Germany that are subject to state control, including shares of German mortgage banks to an amount never exceeding three-fourths of their market value; interest-bearing non-transferable bonds of foreign states, and foreign railway priority bonds, covered by state security, in amounts not exceeding 50 per cent of their market value; bills of exchange of recognized soundness, after deducting at least 5 per cent of their market value; and pledges of native merchandise, in amounts within two-thirds of their value.

d. To negotiate collections for the account of individuals, institutions, and governing boards; and upon security, as before mentioned, to furnish payments, and make orders or conveyances on the branch banks or on correspondents.

e. Upon prior security, to buy on behalf of outside parties, effects of all kinds, including the precious metals; and after delivery to sell the same.

f. To receive money for circulation or on deposit, with or without interest, the sum of interest-bearing deposits not to exceed that of the capital stock and reserve fund.

g. To accept the custody or other management of objects of value.

Besides the Imperial Bank there are in Germany eight very large and powerful banking institutions and a considerable number of smaller and less powerful ones. The eight great ones have each its head office in Berlin, and connections, through branches, agencies, and controlled institutions, in other parts of the Empire, the German colonies, and foreign countries. Together they control about eighty per cent of the entire banking capital of the Empire. In reality they are federations of banking institutions, many of which were once independent, and some of which were promoted and established in the interests of the group.

While these eight institutions are primarily engaged in commercial banking, they are also promoters on a large scale of German industry and commerce, both at home and abroad. Through interlocking directorates, stock ownership, and in other ways, they are closely allied with the leading industrial and transportation interests of the Empire, and they have been and are leaders in the promotion of these interests in other parts of the world, notably in the Orient, South America, and Africa. They are, therefore, leaders on the stock as well as the discount markets of the country, and are widely influential in investment as well as commercial banking affairs.

These, as well as the other commercial banks, consisting for the most part of local institutions and those catering to special interests, use the Imperial Bank for rediscounts, for transfers of funds between different parts of the country, and as a depository for surplus funds. They do not normally keep on hand more cash than is needed for till purposes. Being in easy reach of an office of the Imperial Bank, supplies can be obtained at any time by checks drawn against credit balances or through rediscounts of commercial bills. Special accounts are carried for transfer purposes and are used even in the transfer of funds between different offices of the same institution.

On account of its right to issue notes against commercial securities, the Imperial Bank has the power to meet the demands made upon it and to supply the country with an elastic medium of exchange. The levy of a tax upon the excess of the issues above a prescribed maximum prevents perfect elasticity, unless this maximum be kept above the highest point which the circulation would normally reach, since the actual levy of the tax forces the rate of discount to such a point as to seriously restrict commercial operations.

However, since the line between commercial and investment banking is not drawn by the great Berlin banks with the care that is desirable, and since they have been able at times, especially on account of their foreign connections, to embarrass the Imperial Bank in its efforts to maintain adequate specie reserves, such a tax is probably a desirable safeguard against over-expansion of credit.

5. The Canadian System

In important respects the Canadian banking system differs from those of the European countries which have been described and from that of the United States. It consists of a varying number of relatively large institutions, each with several offices administered from a common center, but without a central bank. For some time the total number has decreased, since 1900 from thirty-six to twenty-seven, in spite of the fact that the Canadian law, like that of the United States, provides for the formation of new banks at any time, on compliance with certain prescribed conditions, including a subscribed capital of at least $500,000 and a paid-up capital of at least $250,000. The number of branches, however, has increased rapidly, much more rapidly than the population.

The most noteworthy legal provisions pertaining to the banking business in Canada concern note issues and loans and discounts. Regarding the establishment of branches, the amount, and, with one exception, the composition of the reserves, and many other matters carefully regulated by law in the United States, Canadian bankers are left free to follow their own judgment. Neither is there public examination of banks in Canada. Reports must be regularly made to the Minister of Finance, and he may call for special reports whenever he desires so to do; but neither he nor any other public officer has the right to examine a bank's books or to quiz its officers or directors. In contrast with banking legislation in the United States, another peculiar feature of Canadian law is the incorporation of the Canadian Bankers' Association, an organization resembling in essentials the American Bankers' Association, and the assignment to it of important functions

70

connected with the issue of notes and the winding up of the affairs of failed banks.

Regarding note issues, the chief provisions of the Canadian law are as follows: Each bank is permitted at any time to issue circulating notes to the amount of its capital stock, and between October 1 and January 1 an additional amount, equal to fifteen per cent of its combined capital and surplus, may be issued on payment of a tax to be assessed by the Governor in Council, not to exceed five per cent per annum. The notes are a first lien on all the assets of the bank that issued them, and must be redeemed on demand at the head office and at such other places as are designated by a committee of public officials known as the Treasury Board. As such redemption centers, this board has named Toronto, Montreal, Halifax, Winnipeg, Victoria, St. John, and Charlottetown. Each bank must also deposit with the Minister of Finance a sum of money equal to five per cent of its average circulation. The aggregate of the amounts thus deposited by all the banks is known as the "circulation redemption fund," and may be used in the redemption of the notes of a failed bank. In case the fund is so used, and the liquidated assets of the bank prove to be inadequate for its complete replenishment, a tax sufficient to meet the deficit is levied on the solvent banks in proportion to their circulation.

Regarding loans and discounts, the law aims rather to protect than to restrict the operations of the banks. They may "deal in, discount, and lend money, and make advances upon the security of, and may take as collateral security for any loans, ... bills of exchange, promissory notes, and other negotiable securities, or the stocks, bonds, debentures, and obligations of municipal and other corporations, whether secured by mortgage or otherwise, or Dominion, provincial, British, foreign, and other public securities." The only important restriction placed upon their loaning activities is the prohibition of making advances on the security of landed or other immovable property.

In making loans to wholesale dealers and shippers of produce, the law safeguards the banks by allowing them to take a blanket lien on the goods dealt in by the borrower. This lien applies not only to the goods in possession at the date of making the loan, but to any others which may be substituted for them or manufactured out of them. This lien is prior to that of any other unpaid vendor, except one acquired before the bank's lien was established.

The chief officers of a Canadian bank are the general manager, the chief accountant, the superintendent of branches, the inspector, and the secretary, all connected with the head office, and the managers of the branches.

The general manager is the chief executive and the chief in authority. While he is subject to the board of directors, on account of his wide experience and knowledge his judgment is usually followed. The other officers are appointed by him with the approval of the board, but, almost without exception, from persons who have served the bank in subordinate capacities. The general manager himself is nearly always a man who has passed through the hierarchy of positions from the bottom up, and is therefore thoroughly familiar with every detail of the bank's business and history. The inspector has charge of the examination of the branches, and this work is so carefully and thoroughly done that examination by public officials is not considered necessary, or regarded as desirable by most Canadian bankers. Regarding this matter, however, there are differences of opinion, and changes in the near future are not improbable. The managers of the branches are in strict subordination to the authority of the general manager, though they are necessarily allowed a large amount of discretionary authority in matters pertaining to the branch over which they preside. Unless prevented by distance, they are in daily communication with the head office or with one of its representatives.

In the operation of the Canadian system, noteworthy features are the methods of controlling credits, of managing the issues and the reserves, and of securing unity or at least harmony of action. It is the usual practice in Canada for a business man to do all his banking with one institution. This practice is rendered possible because most of the banks are large enough to take proper care of almost any business establishment in the Dominion, and because experience has demonstrated its wisdom.

The banks compete vigorously for new business but do not attempt to attract one anothers' customers. Indeed a customer who desires to change his banking connections is looked upon with suspicion and is subjected to a very careful examination by the bank that is asked to take him on, including a careful discussion of all the aspects of the matter with the bank he desires to leave. The result of this practice is that a man's banker is thoroughly familiar with his affairs, especially his credit relations, and at the same time feels under obligations to render him such support and guidance as he deserves. On account of this practice, also, commercial paper brokerage does not flourish in Canada.

The notes of the Canadian banks constitute practically all of the hand-to-hand money of the country in denominations above two dollars. The one and two dollar denominations are supplied by Dominion notes—all but $30,000,000 of which are represented by gold coin or bullion—and the lower denominations by subsidiary silver supplied by the government.

Each bank pays out its notes freely to supply the cash demands of its customers, and receives from them on deposit, without hesitation or depreciation, the notes of other banks as well as its own. The former, however, are either sent in for redemption as soon as received or used in making payments to the banks which issued them. Thus notes are cleared as readily as checks and the volume in circulation expands and contracts in automatic response to business needs. The fact that these notes are neither legal tender nor guaranteed by the government does not interfere with their circulation—daily clearings, the first lien on assets, and the redemption fund amply protecting holders against the possibility of loss—but does prevent their being hoarded as reserves or for any other purpose and thus contributes towards their elasticity.

The connection now established by law between the maximum volume of bank note issues and the capitalization of the banks renders necessary the increase of the latter in correspondence with the expansion of commerce in order to prevent a contraction of credit. Present law, however, does not provide for such an increase. It is left to the voluntary action of the banks, which seem inclined to increase surplus funds rather than capital. The permission granted in 1908 to extend issues beyond the amount of capital during the crop moving season, on payment of a tax, is a makeshift and not a solution of the difficulty, since a tax on issues is a means of forcing contraction of credit and not of adjusting issues to legitimate needs.

Since Canadian banks are able to meet the greater part of the public demand for hand-to-hand money by means of their own notes, they do not need to carry in their vaults large amounts of gold and silver coin and Dominion notes. They keep on hand only so much as experience indicates they are likely to be called upon to supply to their customers, plus a reasonable margin for safety and for the payment of clearing house balances. The greater part of their reserves consists of balances in banks outside of Canada, especially in the United States and England, call loans in New York City, and easily salable securities. In case of an emergency of any kind these resources may be transformed into gold or their customers supplied with foreign exchange, which is often as much or even more needed. Gold can at any time be exchanged for Dominion notes if that is the currency wanted.

The lack of a central bank and of a rediscount market is to a degree compensated by unity of action among the banks. This is the result not so much of law as of conditions, among which the most important are: the fact that the six largest banks do fifty per cent of the business and that one of these, the Bank of Montreal, holds most of the deposits of the government and is generally spoken of as the government bank; the fact that the general managers are experts, in first-hand touch through their branches with business conditions in Canada and other parts of the world, and in possession of the same data concerning these conditions, and through the same kind of acquired skill and similar experiences likely to draw the same or at least similar conclusions from this data; common interests in the prosperity of the country and in the prevention of speculative excesses and mutual interdependence in the successful conduct of their everyday business as well as in times of emergency and stress: and the Bankers' Association, which through its journal gives authoritative expression to the best banking opinion and actually acts for the banks in many matters of common interest. To what extent this community of action takes the form of rediscounts for each other in ordinary times it is impossible for an outsider to say, but that it is operative in times of stress is indicated by the manner in which the failures of the Bank of Ontario in 1906 and the Sovereign Bank in 1908 were handled.

In both of these cases the public was protected against loss and panic was averted by the cooperative action of the other banks in assuming the obligations of these institutions to the public, and in winding up their affairs in such a manner as to occasion little disturbance.

While Canadian banks are free to carry on investment as well as commercial banking operations, their published reports indicate that they take care to avoid confusion of the two, or the infringement of one upon the other. Their holdings of investment securities are kept well within the limits set by their aggregate capital, surplus, and savings funds, and their method of handling commercial business, based as it is on accurate knowledge of their customer's operations and upon the lien upon produce heretofore described, prevents their acceptance, through ignorance, of investment securities under commercial disguise.

CHAPTER VI

Investment Banking

In the economy of nations the encouragement and promotion of saving and the accumulation, distribution, and investment of capital are as essential as the conduct of exchanges, but the performance of these functions has not been segregated and institutionalized to the same extent as has commercial banking. Vast amounts of capital are invested directly by the people to whom it belongs without the aid of middlemen and large amounts are also invested through brokers of one kind and another who can hardly be classed as bankers. The most important types of institutions which have been developed in connection with these functions are savings banks, trust companies, bond houses and investment companies, land banks, and stock exchanges.

1. Saving and Savings Institutions

Saving is an individual matter for which the essential conditions are the development of the instinct to make provision against uncertainties of future income and to better the material condition of one's self and family, and a surplus of income above necessary daily expenditures. In order to secure the realization of these conditions to as great an extent as possible, many agencies cooperate in all modern nations, among them savings institutions. Included among these are various forms of provident associations, sometimes independently organized and sometimes connected with other organizations, insurance associations of many kinds, building and loan societies, and savings banks.

The need for savings institutions varies greatly among the different nations and among different classes of people in the same nation. Among people of great wealth the surplus of income above expenditures is so great that large savings can hardly be avoided, and among all the well-to-do classes

76

the margin from which savings are possible is sufficiently large and the desire to save sufficiently great to insure large accumulations of capital. Among these classes there is little or no need for institutions designed primarily for the development of the saving instinct. What they need are institutions for the safe keeping, accumulation, and investment of the savings which they are constantly making. The principal work of savings institutions, therefore, pertains to the classes of people who are not well-to-do and who need encouragement and help in their efforts to improve their material condition, if they are so inclined, and stimulus to make such efforts, if they are not so inclined.

The means available to savings institutions for the accomplishment of these ends are the urging of the importance of saving upon the attention of people who do not adequately appreciate it, the placing at their easy disposal of facilities for making savings when they have the ability and inclination to save, and the application of pressure of various kinds to compel or induce saving.

In the application of these means the methods employed by the various groups of institutions mentioned differ widely and they are efficient in different degrees, partly because they have other objects in view besides the promotion of saving and partly because they deal with different classes of people. Savings banks constitute the only group to which the term bank can properly be applied and consequently the only one to which attention will here be given.

In a book entitled, *Savings and Savings Institutions*, written by Professor Hamilton of Syracuse University, the following definition is given:[A]

Savings banks are institutions established by public authority, or by private persons, in order to encourage habits of saving by affording special security to owners of deposits, and by the payment of interest to the full extent of the net earnings, less whatever reserve the management may deem expedient for a safety fund; and in furtherance of this purpose bank offices are located at places where they are calculated to encourage savings among those persons who most need such encouragement.

[A] Pages 161 and 162.

Professor Hamilton classifies these institutions as trustee, cooperative, municipal, and postal savings banks. In the first group he places institutions managed by boards of philanthropically inclined persons who serve without pay; in the second, those managed cooperatively by the people who make use of them; in the third, those established and administered by municipalities; and in the fourth, those connected with the post-office departments of governments. The strength of trustee savings banks lies in the comparatively low costs of their administration and in the fact that in their investments they are likely to enjoy the advantages of the judgment and enthusiasm of people skilled in the investment business; that of cooperative savings banks, in their adaptability to the special needs of their constituents and in the education which cooperative administration involves; and that of municipal, and especially of postal savings banks, in their capacity to place their services within the easy reach of all who need them and in the confidence which their public character inspires.

In the investment of the funds intrusted to savings banks, safety and as large returns as are consistent with it, rather than ease of liquidation, are the prime considerations, and hence they usually take the form of high grade investment securities rather than of commercial paper. Their deposits are usually subject to withdrawal only after due notice, and, being savings deposits, their withdrawal usually follows only after the lapse of a considerable period of time.

The purpose of their withdrawal is frequently investment and this is sometimes made through the agency of the bank which held the deposit and may involve merely a transfer of securities.

Outside of the New England and middle states, savings banks were rare in this country previous to the inauguration of our postal savings bank system in 1911. The explanation of this condition is doubtless to be found chiefly in the wide extension of private, state, and national banks, and trust companies, practically all of which conduct savings departments and solicit the patronage of savers. These institutions have coveted this field and have not encouraged the establishment of savings banks. There is reason to believe, however, that they have not worked the field as thoroughly as savings banks would have done and that, on account of the dominance of their other interests, they are not as well fitted as savings banks to work the field

78

thoroughly. Moreover it is probable that they are not able to pay as high a rate on deposits as well conducted savings banks would be able to pay. There seems, therefore, to be room, and probably need, here for the development of savings banks of some at least, if not all, of the types above described.

2. Trust Companies

Within a comparatively short period of time the trust company has developed into an institution of prime importance in the United States. In the beginning of its history it was, as its name implies, simply an institution for the administration of trusts of various kinds, such as the execution of wills, the guardianship of minors and other dependent persons, the administration of the estates of persons either unable or unwilling to administer them for themselves, and trusteeship under corporate mortgages, especially those of railroads. In the latter capacity they became mortgagees in trust for bondholders, registering the bonds, collecting the interest as it became due, paying the bonds at maturity, and in case of default taking the legal steps which were necessary for the protection of the bondholders.

The execution of these trusts involved in most cases the custody and investment of funds, so that investment banking became a part of their business almost from the beginning, and, in time, in states in which the laws passed for their regulation did not prevent, they added commercial banking to their other functions. In some cases they have also become promoters of enterprises, taking the initiative in the organization of corporations for various industrial and commercial purposes. In New York City, and in individual cases in some other large cities, the commercial end of the business has become the dominant one; in the former case on account of the ability of these companies, unrestricted by certain laws applying to state and national banks, to offer to commercial customers better terms than their competitors. In most states, however, especially in the large cities in which they chiefly flourish, trust companies have become primarily investment banking institutions, their other functions being carried on as side lines and assuming, of course, in some cases greater importance than in others.

Since they are still in the early stages of their development, the status of trust companies in the banking system of the United States is not yet definitely determined. Legislation concerning them varies considerably in different states, as do also their relations with other banking institutions. The competitive character of these relations has resulted in some cases in legislation which has aimed to differentiate and define the various functions which all these institutions perform, and to prescribe the conditions under which each one or each group must be performed, regardless of the way in which they are combined, and in others, in their practical consolidation with national or state banks, or both, through community of stock ownership, interlocking directorates, etc.

From the point of view of the convenience of the public there are advantages in the combination of all the banking functions in a single institution, and the success of trust companies to some extent has been due to this cause, but they have also profited from the unequal competition which exemption from certain limitations imposed on state and national banks has enabled them to enjoy. The removal of the conditions which result in this unequal competition, a process already in progress and likely to continue to completion, will reveal the strength of the advantages of combination versus specialization of functions. Previous to such a revelation it will be impossible to determine whether or not the trust company form of organization is destined to become the dominant one.

3. Bond Houses and Investment Companies

A large part of the business of investment banking in the United States is conducted by corporations and firms organized for the purpose of buying and selling investment securities, especially bonds and mortgages. Rarely, if ever, do these concerns conduct savings accounts. Ordinarily they confine their attention exclusively to the investment end of the business and act in the capacity of jobbers, or brokers, or both.

Within the investment field some of them specialize closely and others deal in a wide range of securities. The specialties most frequently followed are government, state, and municipal bonds, railroad bonds, public service securities, timber bonds, irrigation bonds, and real estate mortgages. Specialization involves the development of expert knowledge of the class of securities dealt in and thus of special serviceableness to both investors and the promoters of the enterprises or the public bodies which issue the securities. These specialists sometimes serve as middlemen between the issuers of securities and other investment banks, as well as between them and the real owners of the capital invested, their expert knowledge being of service to the former as well as the latter.

Until recently there have been few attempts to regulate the operation of these institutions by law, but the fraudulent practices of some of them, and the ignorance and weakness of perhaps the majority of investors, have recently created in some quarters a strong public sentiment in favor of such regulation. In several states legislation has resulted, of which the most noteworthy is the so-called "blue sky laws" of Kansas and some other states.

In details these laws differ widely from one another, but they are alike in that they impose upon some branch of the state government the obligation of supervising both companies which issue securities and those which offer securities for sale. The Kansas law, the first of this kind passed in the United States, has been considered too drastic by most of the companies that have attempted to operate under it, but the Wisconsin law, which went into effect October 1, 1913, is looked upon with more favor.

In formulating these and other laws for the proper regulation of these concerns, it has been found difficult to provide adequate protection to the investing public without unduly hampering the issue and negotiation of securities, but this difficulty should, and in time doubtless will, be overcome. A free and open market for bonds, stocks, and other evidences of indebtedness is essential to freedom of enterprise and mobility of capital, which are in turn essential to the economic prosperity of any country. On the other hand, investors undoubtedly need and deserve the protection of the state against misrepresentation and fraud. It is practically impossible for them in many, perhaps in most, cases to obtain the information necessary for self-protection. The matters and conditions to be dealt with in such legislation are so complex and subject to such frequent change that laws are apt to be imperfect, inefficient, or obstructive. It seems probable that those which do not attempt to be specific and detailed, but give wide powers and discretion to administrative boards or commissions, are most likely to be successful.

4. Land Banks

In Europe an important group of institutions has developed for the supplying of agriculture and the building industries with the capital needed in their operations. The greatest number and variety of these are in Germany, in which their development has been continuous since the days of Frederick the Great.

In order to assist in the recuperation of his kingdom from the devastation caused by the Seven Years' War, Frederick caused the land owners of certain provinces to be organized into associations called Landschaften, which were authorized to issue mortgage bonds on the joint security of the lands of all the members of the association in exchange for mortgages on the lands of individual members who needed funds for the improvement of their estates. These mortgages were made payable to the association in the form of small annuities, to which were added the interest paid on the bonds and an increment for the payment of the expenses of the association.

These associations were governed by the members through a general assembly, representative boards, and elected officers, and were supervised by the state and carefully regulated by law. Regulations were carefully worked out pertaining to the ratio that the loan should bear to the value of the estate mortgaged, methods of valuation, ways and means of maintaining an equilibrium between the bonds issued and the mortgages held, the treatment of defaulting members, etc., etc. Machinery for the sale of the mortgage bonds delivered to members was also created, and in some cases later on these sales were made directly by the associations themselves, and cash paid to the maker of the mortgages.

Five of these original Landschaften have continued to the present day, and others modeled after them were subsequently established. In 1909 in all Germany twenty-five were in operation, of which eighteen were in Prussia. The newer ones have not in all respects followed their models. Unlike the original five, membership in them is not limited to the nobility and is not compulsory; the liability of the members for the payment of the bonds issued has in some cases been limited to a percentage of the total; the loans are usually paid in cash; and the bonds are sold directly by the associations; but the principles of mutual liability and mutual control which were basic in the old organizations have not been violated in any case. Both old and new are organized in the interests of borrowers on real estate mortgage security, and aim to secure funds for these on the lowest possible terms and for long periods of time, by making the security offered the lenders greater than any single borrower could supply.

The degree of their success is indicated by the fact that in 1909 the amount of their outstanding mortgage loans amounted to nearly a billion dollars, and that their mortgage bonds rank on the exchanges with Prussian state bonds and have at times outranked them.

Another type of land bank appeared in the early part of the nineteenth century as a result of the movement for the freeing of the serfs and their transformation into freehold peasants. The lands of these cultivators were burdened with a variety of feudal dues and charges which had to be commuted before they could become freeholds. In order to facilitate this process banks were established which assumed the obligations of a peasant towards his feudal superior in return for a mortgage on his holding, repayable with interest in the form of an annuity, and in amount equal to the sum to be paid to the feudal superior for the total extinguishment of all feudal obligations.

Some of these banks were established and administered by states, provinces, and communes, and some by private parties. The public ones obtained the funds they needed partly from subsidies and partly from the sale of guaranteed mortgage bonds and the private ones wholly from the sale of mortgage bonds.

The completion of the work for which these banks were originally established put an end to their development about 1883, but similar institutions have since been established in Prussia to assist colonists in the purchase and equipment of their farms, and in central and western Germany to promote general agricultural and urban real estate operations. The colonists sent into Poland for the Germanization of that province were in this way assisted by the Prussian government, and in some parts of Germany the same means have been employed for the purpose of aiding in the process of breaking up large estates into small holdings, in the construction of dikes, roads, and reservoirs, and in changing the courses of streams.

Next to the Landschaften the most important intermediaries between capitalists and investors in real estate in Germany are the so-called Hypothekenaktienbanken, or joint-stock mortgage banks. These are private corporations, capitalized by the sale of stock shares to the general public, and controlled by their stockholders through directorates, like industrial corporations the world over. Their business is the making of long-period loans on real estate security, and the funds thus employed are obtained by the sale of mortgage bonds secured by the real estate mortgages in which the proceeds are invested and by their own capital, surplus, and other funds.

They differ from the Landschaften in that they are not cooperative or mutual institutions, but strictly business enterprises run in the interests of their stockholders. Their primary aim is to earn dividends rather than to secure the lowest possible loan rates and other favorable terms for borrowers. As a matter of fact they are forced by competition and by the principles of good business to make loans at reasonable rates and on favorable terms regarding repayment and other matters, and they successfully compete with the Landschaften and other cooperative credit institutions of Germany. Their mortgage loans are usually made repayable on the annuity plan, one-half per cent each year being the common rate of payment, and they loan about the same percentage of the value of the lands mortgaged, as do the Landschaften and other land banks, and the rate of interest charged is the market rate, into the determination of which, of course, the competition of all other institutions enter.

While these institutions loan in the aggregate enormous sums on farm property, their chief field of operations is urban real estate, and particularly the industry of residence, or as we would call it in this country, apartment-house construction. It is on this account that the period of their most rapid development coincides with that of the recent rapid industrial and commercial development of Germany, which dates back only to the establishment of the Empire in 1870. Most of them began operations in the decade 1862-1872, but the most rapid growth in the magnitude and scope of their business operations has come in recent years.

In 1899 there were forty institutions of this kind in operation in the German Empire. The number at the present time is probably considerably greater, since for obvious reasons combinations among them are not promoted by the same kind of economic pressure that in recent years has operated so efficiently in Germany in the field of commercial banking.

Two other groups of German institutions merit attention in this connection, namely, the so-called Schulze-Delitzsch and the Raiffeisen Credit Associations.

The Schulze-Delitzsch societies were the direct outcome of the period of dearth and famine through which Germany passed in the years immediately preceding the revolution of 1848. The first one was not a credit association, but a cooperative buying society, organized by a local judge named Schulze for the aid of his needy neighbors of the small trading class in the town of Delitzsch. In 1850 a credit association on the same plan was organized. Others followed, in rapid succession in and after the seventies, until at the present time they are numbered by the thousands and their members by millions, and they are scattered throughout the entire empire.

The principle of their organization is the association of a comparatively small group of neighbors, or of people who know one another well, or who may easily come to know one another well, by each making a contribution to a common fund to be loaned out to individuals on personal security chiefly, and which, together with the credit of the entire group, may be made the basis of security for larger funds to be borrowed on the open market. They are carefully organized on the cooperative principle, each member having an equal voice in a general assembly which chooses a board of directors and a small administrative board, to which is intrusted the actual management and administration of the affairs of the society.

Loans are made to members only, usually for short periods of time, on the personal security of the borrower and of others who are willing to vouch for him, and on the unusually favorable terms which the credit of the entire organization and very low costs of administration render possible. The knowledge which each member has of the character and business methods of his fellow members who borrow, and of the use to which borrowed funds are put, and the stake which each one has in the financial stability and success of the organization, bring the percentage of losses to a very low figure, and make it possible for these societies to grant their members maximum accommodations at minimum prices.

To the funds accumulated from initiation fees, membership dues and the sale of the associations' credit have been added, in constantly increasing amounts in recent years, the savings of the members themselves. Many societies have such an amount of funds intrusted to them in this way that they are not only entirely freed from the necessity of borrowing, but are obliged to seek opportunities for investment outside their own group.

This condition of affairs, in addition to many other common interests, led to the federation of the Schulze-Delitzsch societies into larger groups, and these in turn into state and national associations, through which surplus funds in one could be made to serve the needs of others inadequately supplied, and through which all the societies could be brought into efficient connection with the general money market of the country. For a number of years these federated societies conducted a large central institution, first in Frankfurt and afterwards in Berlin, known as the Deutsche Genossenschaftsbank. In 1904, however, this institution was absorbed by the Dresdener Bank, one of the eight great private banking corporations of Germany, which now serves as the central agency for all these societies.

The membership of these associations is not restricted to any class of persons, and they actually include a very large number of small farmers. An inquiry made in 1885 showed that in 545 of them, with a total membership of 270,808, there were 72,994 farmers, and that one-fifth of the total loans of these associations were made to this class of their members. They must, therefore, be numbered among the land banks of the Empire, or at least among the institutions which are helping to solve the credit problem for the agricultural classes.

The Raiffeisen societies resemble the Schulze-Delitzsch in many particulars and differ from them in others. Like them they are strictly cooperative in character, and, when organized for credit purposes, designed to supply members with loans on the most favorable possible terms. Their development was also due to the hard economic conditions of the period immediately succeeding the revolution in 1848.

They differ from the Schulze-Delitzsch societies chiefly in the following particulars: They charge no initiation fees and do not rely to the same extent on the proceeds of the sale of shares, the amount of which they place at a very low figure, often the lowest permitted by law; they make long-period as well as short-period loans, indeed the former chiefly; they do not pay dividends on their share capital, but instead put all profits into reserve funds or prevent their accumulation by keeping the loan rates low; they exercise more care than do the Schulze-Delitzsch associations to keep their societies small, laying great emphasis upon the importance of personal acquaintance between members and thus upon mutual watchfulness; and, in their origin, they were peasant organizations pure and simple, and hence more strictly land banks.

Their founder, F. W. Raiffeisen, Burgomeister of a small village in Westphalia, Prussia, wanted to rescue the poor peasants of his and other districts from the clutches of the usurers, into whose hands they had fallen and by whom they were being exploited in a most shameful manner. Since it was loans that these people needed and since their cash resources were always very low and in many cases nil, he felt that to require, as a condition of membership, entrance fees and the purchase of one or more shares of stock, however small, would be fatal to the success of his plans. He also firmly believed that in the integrity, industry, frugality, and agricultural skill of these people was the basis for sound credit and that cooperation was a means by which these elements of sound credit could be made available and attractive on the money market. At the beginning, therefore, no entrance fees or share subscriptions were required. Later Prussian law made share subscriptions compulsory and they were, of course, introduced, but they were made so low, and the acquisition of the money for their purchase so easy, that they have not been a serious obstacle.

From the beginning Raiffeisen invited to membership in his societies the well-to-do and substantial people as well as peasants. Of course these people did not require the society for the satisfaction of their own credit needs, but Raiffeisen saw that they would greatly strengthen the credit of the societies and he was able to appeal to them on philanthropic grounds. This class of people have a leading part in the administration of the societies of which they are members and have contributed greatly to their success.

At the outset the Raiffeisen societies had to rely chiefly on borrowing for the acquisition of the capital needed, but with time and success savings deposits, surplus funds accumulated out of profits, and lastly the proceeds of the sale of shares have played an increasing rôle. At the present time many societies are not obliged to borrow at all, and not a few have surplus funds which are placed at the disposition of other societies which are still obliged to borrow.

Like the Schulze-Delitzsch societies the Raiffeisen associations have federated. At present there are thirteen so-called unions, and at the head of all is a central bank with head office at Berlin and branches at Königsberg, Danzig, Breslau, Cassel, Frankfurt, Coblenz, Brunzwick, Strassburg, Nuremberg, Posen, and Ludwigshafen. The central bank is a joint-stock company, organized on the principle of limited liability, the stock of which is owned by the local societies. It formerly had close relations with the Imperial Bank, but is now associated with the so-called Centralgenossenschaftskassa, endowed by the state of Prussia, in such a way that advances and discounts are extended to it on favorable terms.

The Raiffeisen societies rival the Schulze-Delitzsch in the rapidity of their growth and in the rôle they play in the economic life of modern Germany. In 1908 they numbered 5,047, of which 4,340 were credit associations. The collective balance sheets of these societies in 1907 showed 490,734,834 marks assets, 489,234,357 marks liabilities, and a membership of 405,819.

While Germany was the pioneer in the establishment of land credit institutions, and while such institutions have attained a greater variety of form and a higher degree of perfection in that country than in any other, other countries have advanced along similar lines and now have institutions and a fund of experience well worthy of study. The institutions of Germany have in most cases served as models in these other countries, the mortgage banks and the Schulze-Delitzsch and Raiffeisen societies having been most frequently copied. These models have been adapted to foreign conditions and modified in interesting and instructive ways as well as copied without essential change.

Among the mortgage banks developed outside of Germany the Crédit Foncier of France is especially noteworthy. In its organization it was modeled after the Bank of France and is second only to that institution in the magnitude of its operations and the scope of its influence. Its head office is in Paris and it has at least one branch in each department. Its capital stock owned by private parties amounts to about $40,000,000, its surplus to over $4,000,000, its loans secured by mortgage to over $400,000,000, and its total resources to about $1,000,000,000.

Like the German mortgage banks, it secures the greater part of its loan funds through the issue of mortgage bonds and a large percentage of its loans are made on mortgage security for long periods of time and are repayable on the annuity plan. However, it transacts a greater variety of business than does the typical mortgage bank of Germany. It loans on city and farm real estate and to communes, and it transacts a large commercial banking business, though this is distinctly a side issue, incorporated with its other business in order to give profitable employment to funds, sometimes large in amount, which are temporarily on hand awaiting investment.

At various times it has absorbed competing institutions and at times it has established collateral institutions to transact lines of business for which its own constitution and legal limitations did not fit it. Among these the most important are the Crédit Agricole and the Foncier Algierienne. It was obliged ultimately to absorb and liquidate the former, but the latter still flourishes in the colony of Algiers.

Mortgage banks have also gained a footing in most of the other countries of continental Europe. In Italy they passed through a period of storm and stress, owing to their connection with the issue banks of that country and the consequent confusion between commercial and investment banking which resulted, but they have recently been established on an independent basis and are now developing along right lines and with apparent success.

The Schulze-Delitzsch and Raiffeisen societies have been imitated in Austria, Hungary, Belgium, Switzerland, and, to some extent, in France and India. The so-called "Banche Populari" and "Casse Rurali" of Italy are respectively modified forms of these two German types, and rank among the most important means employed in that country for the improvement of the condition of the peasants and small tradesmen. State, provincial, and communal aid for these institutions has been more frequently evoked and more extensively employed outside than inside of Germany, and other important modifications of the German prototypes have been made in Italy and elsewhere.

5. Stock Exchanges

An essential part of the machinery of investment banking is the stock exchange. This is a place where the buyers and sellers of securities or their agents regularly meet for the transaction of business. It may be a portion of a street or a market place or a room in a building. A fully equipped modern exchange contains a large room equipped with telegraphic and telephonic communication with the most important parts of the country in which it is located and of the world, with apparatus for registering prices and easily communicating information to its members, and with the offices needed for the accommodation of the clerks and other employees required. Either by posts or in some other manner the precise places in it in which each security or group of securities is to be dealt in is also usually indicated.

The purpose of the stock exchange is to facilitate and to regulate dealings in securities. It facilitates such dealings by providing as nearly perfect means as is possible for putting buyers and sellers into communication with each other, and for collecting and making available to them the information they need. To this end they provide for daily meetings at fixed hours; they make and publish lists of the securities dealt in; they speedily record and, through the telegraph and the telephone, communicate to all quarters of the globe the prices at which securities change hands; and through the meeting

90

room equipped as before described they make it possible for buyers and sellers, no matter where located, to communicate with each other in a very short period to time. They regulate such dealings by establishing and rigidly enforcing rules and regulations for listing, transferring, clearing, and paying for securities and for other matters pertaining to the conduct of their members.

These institutions serve investment banks as well as private investors, constituting the machinery which connects them all. They thus enlarge the area and scope of the markets for securities, and greatly increase the mobility of capital. Without them the surplus savings of one locality would only very slowly and with difficulty find their way to other localities where they are needed, with the result that capital would lie idle or be very inefficiently employed in some places while in others natural and human resources would be undeveloped or very inefficiently developed.

Existing stock exchanges differ considerably in the manner in which they are organized and managed, in methods of doing business, and in the scope of their operations. Some of them are incorporated and others unincorporated; some restrict their membership to a prescribed number, others admit as many as are able and willing to comply with the conditions imposed; some are local in their scope, some national, and others international. In this country all the exchanges deal in local securities chiefly, except the one in New York City, which is national in its scope. The London exchange does a larger business in international securities than any other, but the Paris and Berlin exchanges, as well as those located at the other important European capitals, and the one at New York share in it to a greater or less degree.

Stock exchanges have suffered in reputation, and their real functions and merits have been obscured by the abuses to which they have been subjected. Connected with their legitimate business of facilitating the investment of capital, various forms of speculation have developed which in some cases have degenerated into gambling pure and simple. The better managed ones have striven to rid themselves of these abuses, and in some countries, notably in Germany, legislative bodies have taken a hand. The results, however, have proved only partially successful.

Some forms of speculation are not only legitimate but necessary in modern business life, and these shade into the illegitimate, unnecessary, and positively harmful forms by such short and easy steps as to render it difficult, and perhaps impossible, to draw a line between the two which can serve as a guide for regulations of an administrative or legislative kind.

6. Some Defects in Our Investment Banking Machinery

A comparison of our investment banking machinery with that of European countries, especially Germany, reveals important differences. Among these the most notable are the wide use there and the almost complete absence here of the following: (a) the resort to cooperation as a means of revealing and making available the basis for credit of large numbers of people who lack capital but could use it to the advantage of themselves and of the nation; (b) the long-period mortgage loan repayable on the annuity plan and the mortgage bond as a means of accumulating capital for such loans; and (c) the cooperation of the state and other public bodies and of capitalists and philanthropically disposed persons in developing the credit possibilities of the masses and in directing the flow of proper portions of the stream of capital in their direction.

In the development of investment banking institutions in this country, individual initiative prompted by self-interest has been the chief, and except in the case of savings banks, the sole motive force. The result is that most of them have been organized in the interests of lenders rather than borrowers and serve best the purposes of big business and of persons already possessed of large credit by virtue of their wealth or their business reputations. Under these conditions, while enormous amounts of capital in the aggregate have been invested in agriculture and urban real estate, the former has suffered relatively in comparison with transportation, manufacturing, and speculation.

Contributory causes in the development of this situation have been the great need for capital for the development of our transportation system, the stimulation of manufactures by high protective duties, and the enormous area of our public domain which was given or sold to settlers on very easy terms. Inasmuch as our transportation system and our manufacturing industries have now attained a high degree of development, our public domain has been nearly exhausted, and land values and the cost of living are rapidly rising, the needs of agriculture are pushing themselves into the foreground, and we are beginning to look to European experience for suggestions regarding the best methods of diverting to that industry a larger part of our rapidly accumulating capital resources.

There are obvious difficulties in the way of the application of cooperation to the solution of the problem of agricultural credit in this country. In spite of the fact that immigration is constantly bringing to us people from the very foreign countries in which cooperative credit associations flourish, our agricultural population is still dominated by the spirit of individualism which has been and is one of our dominant national traits. Our farmers are also more widely scattered than is the case in Europe, and consequently less closely knit together in social units. Their holdings are also larger, their capital needs greater, and their business instincts more highly developed.

There seems to be no good reason, however, why the joint-stock mortgage bank should not flourish here as well as in Europe. It is a purely private business enterprise of the kind with which we are perfectly familiar. The mortgage bond ought to appeal to our investors, many of whom have exhibited a strong predilection for mortgage security and real estate investments, and long-period mortgage loans, repayable on the annuity plan, would meet the needs of many land purchasers and of people who need to invest considerable sums in drainage, irrigation works, etc., better than our present methods. In most, if not all, of our states, trust companies could develop these new lines of finance without prejudice to the other branches of their business.

The use of state, county, and municipal subsidies or credit in enterprises of this kind is rendered difficult, if not impossible, in this country, by strong prejudice against the use of public funds in private enterprises, and in some states by constitutional prohibitions. This prejudice is based upon unfortunate experiences, and is at least partially justified by the laxness of our administrative methods and the prevalence of graft, which expose us to the danger of the improper use of public funds devoted to enterprises of this kind. There is no reason, however, why our states should not take the initiative in the improvement of our investment banking machinery and why private capitalists and philanthropists should not turn some of their energy into this channel.

Suggestion and leadership are needed in this field quite as much as legislation tending to restrict and regulate the operations of existing institutions.

REFERENCES

The following books are comprehensive in character, treating most of the subjects covered in the foregoing chapters:

Macleod, H. D., Theory and Practice of Banking.

Gilbart, J. W., History and Principles of Banking.

Bagehot, Walter, Lombard Street.

Dunbar, Charles F., History and Theory of Banking.

Scott, Wm. A., Money and Banking. Rev. Ed.

White, Horace, Money and Banking.

Fisk, A. K., The Modern Bank.

The subject of clearings and the exchanges are discussed in the following books:

Cannon, J. G., Clearing Houses.

Clare, George, The A, B, C of the Exchanges.

Clare, George, A Money Market Primer and Key to the Foreign Exchanges.

Margraff, A. W., International Exchange.

Escher, F., Foreign Exchange.

The following cover the history and present condition of banking in the leading countries:

Conant, C. A., Modern Banks of Issue.

Knox, J. J., A History of Banking in the United States.

Sumner, Wm. G., A History of Banking in the United States, being Vol. I of a History of Banking in all the leading nations.

Kirkbride & Sterrett, J. E., The Modern Trust Company, Its Functions and Organization.

Breckenridge, R. M., The History of Banking in Canada.

Laughlin, J. L., Editor, Banking Reform.

Johnson, J. F., The Canadian Banking System.

Withers, Hartley, Palgrave, R. H., and others, The English Banking System.

Liesse, A., Evolution of Credit and Banks in France.
National Monetary Commission, The Reichsbank, 1876-1900.
Riesser, J., The German Great Banks and Their Concentration.

On investment banking see:
Wolff, H., People's Banks.
Peters, E. E., Co-operative Credit Associations.
Hamilton, J. H., Saving and Savings Institutions.
Pratt, S. S., The Work of Wall Street.
Conant, C. A., Wall Street and the Country.

INDEX

balance, 16, 18-20, 23, 25;
cooperation in, 166-168;
department in banks, 43, 86;
inflation of, 87;
"line" of, 16, 85, 86;
subsidies, state, county, and municipal, 169;
system, 11-13

Credits, forced liquidation of, 49

Crédit Agricole, 162;
Foncier, 113;
Industrielle et Commercial, 115, 116;
Lyonnais, 115, 116

Crisis, commercial, 19, 31, 88

Currency, 21, 22;
lack of elasticity, 95-97

Debt paying, 13, 14

Debits, 15-18

Demand in foreign exchange, 33, 34

Deposits, 2-4

Depositors, mutual insurance of, 60-62

Discount, defined, 14;
loans and discounts, selection of, 40-43;
loans and rates, 44;
operation of, 13;

103

operations of system, 91-94;
regulations regarding, 52, 54;
secondary, 35-40;
in state banks, 69;
in country banks, 73

Safety, in savings banks, 140;
fund, 56, 57

Savings banks, 6, 9;
defined, 139

Saving and saving institutions, 136-141

Secretary of the Treasury and surplus funds, 88-90

Securities, dealings in the stock exchange, 163, 164

Security, liquid, 53

Silver dollars, 96

Sixty-day bills in foreign exchange, 33, 34

Société Algerienne, 114

Société Generale, 115, 116

State banks, 9, 68-70, 79, 82;
and Federal reserve, 99

St. Louis, central reserve bank, 78;
clearing center, 24

The National Social Science Series

Edited by Frank L. McVey, Ph.D., LL.D.,
President of the
University of North Dakota

Now Ready

MONEY. William A. Scott, Director of the Course in Commerce, and Professor of Political Economy, University of Wisconsin

TAXATION. C. B. Fillebrown, President Massachusetts Single Tax League, Author of *A B C of Taxation*

THE FAMILY AND SOCIETY. John M. Gillette, Professor of Sociology, University of North Dakota

BANKING. William A. Scott

In Preparation

THE CITY. Henry C. Wright

TRUSTS AND COMPETITION. John F. Crowell

THE COST OF LIVING. Walter E. Clark

STATISTICS. W. B. Bailey

BASIS OF COMMERCE. E. V. Robinson

PUBLIC FINANCE. Carl C. Plehn

Each, Fifty Cents Net

A. C. McCLURG & CO., PUBLISHERS, CHICAGO

End of the Book

www.ingramcontent.com/pod-product-compliance
Lightning Source LLC
Chambersburg PA
CBHW051726170526
45167CB00002B/814